Springer Textbooks in Law

Springer Textbooks in Law compiles high-quality educational content aimed at undergraduate and graduate students in all areas of law. All self-contained volumes are authored by accomplished academics and suitable for use in class as well as individual study. Many of them include chapter abstracts, definitions of technical terms, cases and self-assessment exercises, as well as recommended reading sections. This series is an invaluable resource for students and lecturers alike and spans the full range of topics in international and European law, including fundamentals of law and comparative law. Special attention is paid to current and emerging topics such as IT law, intellectual property, human rights as well as dispute resolution, mediation, arbitration – and many more.

Frauke Heidemann

An International Law Perspective on Harry Potter

Explaining Core Principles of
International Law by Testing their
Relevance in the Wizarding World

 Springer

Frauke Heidemann
Dülmen, Germany

ISSN 2509-999X   ISSN 2510-0009   (electronic)
Springer Textbooks in Law
ISBN 978-3-031-57570-9   ISBN 978-3-031-57571-6   (eBook)
https://doi.org/10.1007/978-3-031-57571-6

This Springer imprint is published by the registered company Springer Nature Switzerland AG
The registered company address is: Gewerbestrasse 11, 6330 Cham, Switzerland

If disposing of this product, please recycle the paper.

Preface

When reading the Harry Potter books, have you ever wondered how the worlds of Muggles and wizards coexist? Not just practically, but also legally. Did you ever scratch your head thinking about whether the death eaters were committing crimes against humanity? Have you raised the question whether the members of Dumbledore's Army could be considered child soldiers? If you haven't, that is fine. If you have, it may be a sign that you need to get your nose out of books. But once those questions have been raised, it is difficult to let them go. This book is here to help. It answers the most pressing issues that have kept you up at night. When you are done reading this book, you will not only have had the chance to take a deep dive into the nerdy worlds of Harry Potter and international law, but you will also be guaranteed to never run out of small talk topics—imagine not having to start an awkward conversation about the weather while boring yourself senseless during a house party or cocktail reception, but instead discussing the Dementors of Azkaban being part of a torture scheme by a government's executive body (the Ministry of Magic).

Nevertheless, this book is not merely a fun project, but also a highly useful contribution to academic discourse. It helps test how our international legal regime can deal with unforeseen actors. As we see many rapid changes internationally (only think about the rise in non-state actors), why not test our legal regime by applying it to a totally out-of-the-box concept such as witches and wizards and thus ridding the debates from political factors?[1] Let's be honest, we can all use a break of heated political debates from time to time.

And for the non-lawyers among you, this book might serve as an introduction into a topic otherwise often considered very dull. But be aware, once your interest in the fascinating world of international law is sparked, it is hard to live a life without it. In many ways, it is just as addictive as the relationship you developed with the Harry Potter universe. If you haven't read Harry Potter, but are still interested in reading this book, let me be very honest: there is a huge gap in your general education which

---

[1]Going one step further, consider the potential relevance of this study if the U.S. space force encounters extraterrestrial lifeforms and needs to assess how to engage with them in accordance with its international legal obligations. There are scenarios in which our current realities cannot be fully adapted to the changes we are seeing—so why not get ready for them?

you'll have to close before continuing down this path. So, close this book and do what you should have done years ago: read all Harry Potter books! If you have only seen the movies, shame on you, but it is a start and you may continue.

This journey will take you through the worlds of public international law, international humanitarian law, international criminal law, international human rights law, law of the sea, and air law (yes, stick with me, you can even make air law fascinating if you add flying cars and broomsticks). If at any point you feel that: (a) questions are left unanswered, (b) you would like to share your thoughts, or (c) my argument is wrong, please get in touch with me (in case a and b) or rethink your argument (in case c). No, of course, always get in touch, particularly if you believe that my interpretation of the wizarding world is far-fetched.

Some topics will remain uncovered even though they are highly fascinating. This particularly relates to questions of tax law and economic law (yes, think about the implications of Gringotts as a tax evasion scheme for Muggle-borns)—leaving this for future assessments. Other topics such as national law remain out of scope for now, but have been covered in the works of a wide range of lawyers.[2]

Before we start our journey into the fascinating world of wizardry, it needs to be established how to interpret factual discrepancies that might arise between the books and the movies. Clearly, the English language books have priority given that they are the original works. Thereafter, the movies will be taken into consideration. If neither provides clarity, context can be established through the discussions led at leading platforms such as Pottermore (now Wizarding World of course, but I don't like change and therefore still refer to it the old way). Here, particularly the contributions by J. K. Rowling are essential to provide further details on the wizarding world. Additional works related to the same universe, in particular the Hogwarts book series and the Fantastic Beasts spin-offs, are used to clarify underlying questions about the history of the wizarding world and the interaction between Muggles and wizards— and of course fantastic beasts.

Dülmen, Germany   Frauke Heidemann

---

[2] One such magical work is: Thomas JE, Snyder FG (eds) (2010) The law and Harry Potter. Carolina Academic Press, Durham.

Acknowledgment

Writing a book about international law and Harry Potter sounds like an idea you get after a few too many beers. And that is exactly how the idea for this book came about. A big thank you to Benjamin Wyler for not only being a truly amazing friend, but also for engaging in hours-long discussions about legal questions linked to Harry Potter that eventually led to the idea of writing this book. It has been a few years since the initial idea was born. In the meantime, I had plenty of support from all my dear Potterhead friends who engaged in expert discussions with me, whether during hikes, over a drink, or virtually via Zoom during the lockdown periods. A big thank you to Sarah-Kay Schotte, Sarah Schüpbach, Gina Gutzwiler, Eugenia Kazakova, Aline Renz, Patrick Renz, Martin Wendiggensen as well as Niklas and Julia Heidemann. Your willingness to engage in nerdy discussions with me has made the book what it is.

Contents

Abbreviations

ACHPR	African Charter on Human and People's Rights (Banjul Charter)
ACHR	(Inter-) American Convention on Human Rights
ADIZ	Air Defense Identification Zone
AP	Additional Protocol
ArCHR	Arab Charter on Human Rights
ASA	Air Service Agreement
ASR	Articles on State Responsibility
AWS	Autonomous Weapon System
CAT	Convention against Torture and Other Cruel, Inhuman or Degrading Treatment or Punishment
CEDAW	Convention on the Elimination of All Forms of Discrimination against Women
CoE	Council of Europe
CPED	International Convention for the Protection of All Persons from Enforced Disappearance
CRC	Convention on the Rights of the Child
CRPD	Convention on the Rights of Persons with Disabilities
ECHR	European Convention on Human Rights
ECtHR	European Court of Human Rights
EEZ	Exclusive Economic Zone
EU	European Union
GA	General Assembly
HRC	Human Rights Council
IAC	International Armed Conflict
ICC	International Criminal Court
ICCPR	International Covenant on Civil and Political Rights
ICERD	International Convention on the Elimination of All Forms of Racial Discrimination
ICESCR	International Covenant on Economic, Social and Cultural Rights
ICMW	International Convention on the Protection of the Rights of All Migrant Workers and Members of Their Families
ICJ	International Court of Justice
ICoC	International Code of Conduct

ICoCA	International Code of Conduct Association
ICRC	International Committee of the Red Cross
ICTR	International Criminal Tribunal for Rwanda
ICTY	International Criminal Tribunal for the Former Yugoslavia
IHL	International Humanitarian Law
IHRL	International Human Rights Law
ILC	International Law Commission
IRAC	Issue, Rule, Application and Conclusion
IRMCT	International Residual Mechanism for Criminal Tribunals
JCE	Joint Criminal Enterprise
MACUSA	Magical Congress of the United States of America
MSI	Multi-Stakeholder Initiative
NGO	Non-Governmental Organization
NIAC	Non-International Armed Conflict
OAU	Organization of African Unity
OWL	Ordinary Wizarding Level
PMSC	Private Military and Security Company
POW	Prisoner of War
UK	United Kingdom
UN	United Nations
UNCLOS	UN Convention on the Law of the Sea
UNSC	UN Security Council
UPR	Universal Periodic Review
U.S.	United States
VCLT	Vienna Convention on the Law of Treaties
WCHR	Wizarding Court of Human Rights

Introduction to the World of International Law

Abstract

This chapter provides an overview of what public international law is. It distinguishes between public and private international law and explains the sources of public international law. Finally, the chapter provides an introduction of legal methodology (the equivalent to wand movements, but less impressive to watch).

1.1 Let's Talk About the Basics First

Even Harry first had to go through "The Standard Book of Spells, Grade 1" before venturing on to more complex and fascinating topics such as producing a Patronus charm.[1] So, before we apply our legal theory to the world of Harry Potter, you guessed it, we need to get a basic understanding of legal theory. I will try to keep this more interesting than Professor Binns, being cautiously optimistic that I am not yet a ghost but very much alive and able to read my audience.[2] In case you are a seasoned legal scholar, feel free to skip this section or use it to test your basic knowledge.

Starting with the history of public international law (congrats to all of you who made the link from Professor Binns to this phrase): in the opinion of many scholars, public international law dates back to the Peace Treaty of Westphalia.[3] This peace treaty ended the 30-year-war and was signed in Muenster and Osnabrueck (both

---

[1] See on this the shopping list Harry Potter took to Flourish & Blotts during his first venture to Diagon Alley. More on this in Rowling (1997), Chapter 5: Diagon Alley. Knowing how many editions are out there, I'll only provide reference to the book and relevant chapter.

[2] For those who did not get this reference, read up here: Rowling (1997), Chapter 8: The Potion's Master.

[3] For more detailed assessments about the historical development of public international law, refer to Shaw (2017), pp. 10–23.

cities are very close to where I grew up, adding quite some historical pressure to get it right in this book). It did, however, not only end the 30-year-war but also established that states are sovereign and equal entities. This idea of equal sovereignty is the foundation of public international law. For international relations nerds among you, you might have heard that we are living in an anarchic international society, in which there is no overarching body ruling over all states. This is due to the concept of sovereign states. No one state controls the others (at least in theory, let us leave the debates about power balances to another day), there is no vertical order. This also explains the limitations of the United Nations (UN), which have been frequently decried as a frustratingly powerless talk shop. But as the former UN Secretary General Dag Hammarskjöld rightfully pointed out: "It has been said that the United Nations was not created in order to bring us to heaven, but in order to save us from hell."[4] What does this have to do with public international law? No worries, I do not just want to highlight basic insights into relevant UN quotes. But this quote perfectly explains the relevance of public international law. It will not create heaven. It will never be perfect. Not all states will always adhere to it. The same is true for all laws, otherwise there would be no need for prosecutors, lawyers, judges, policemen. But public international law provides a sense of order in an otherwise anarchic international system. It protects the weak and the small states, acting as a type of shield charm. And it constitutes a basic set of rules applicable to these sovereign legal entities called states.

If you are still unimpressed and do not see how international law impacts you, please have a look at a truly useful compilation by some lawyers, focusing on 100 Ways in which international law shapes our lives.[5] You will be as surprised as Harry was when first stepping from the Leaky Cauldron into Diagon Alley.

So, now that everyone is really excited about international law, let us dive into the core concepts.

1.2   Public International Law vs. Private International Law

We are focusing on public international law in this book. Aside from public international law, there is also private international law. Private international law deals with questions in which international/foreign elements become an issue within the legal system of one country. Public international law creates a separate legal system applicable to states when dealing with one another.[6]

---

[4]More on this famous quote by the former UN Secretary General: https://ask.un.org/loader? fid=11125&type=1&key=6bf400a0db526933d8577cce49f39ad2. I personally even prefer one of the other sentences of the same speech: "The United Nations is not and should not be an organizational strait-jacked on the world or on the independent states which are its Members" as it speaks even more to the fundamental concept of sovereign nation states.

[5]ASIL (2022).

[6]More on private international law in distinction to public international law: Torremans et al. (2017).

To give you a quick example: a British Muggle and a French witch got married in France. The witch failed to disclose the fact that she is a witch and has married the British Muggle in accordance with French Muggle law. After a while, it becomes evident that she is hiding something from him. The British Muggle cannot live with the fact that she hid such a big secret and wants to get a divorce. By now, he is living back in Budleigh Babberton in Britain. To get a divorce, the British court must assess French law given that they were married in France. This is a matter of private international law.[7]

Public international law covers relations between the states themselves on matters such as war and peace, environmental regulation, human rights, international institutions—whatever comes to mind. Public international law—also called *ius gentium* (congrats those of you who took Latin in high school—this is your moment to shine)—will be our focus in this book.

1.3   Why Do We Need Public International Law

As previously mentioned, we live in an anarchic international system, meaning there is no higher authority than states themselves.[8] States are considered sovereign and equal. Sounds great, but what does that mean in practice? If two neighbors within Britain fight because someone has moved their fence a few inches too far (yes, that is a thing) and one of them then mows down the other's garden gnomes and wreaks havoc on the lawn (running the neighbors chances of winning the "All-England Best Kept Suburban Lawn Competition") this goes to court. The court rules and the neighbors have to follow the ruling. If not, well, worst case they go to jail. Though likely not because they destroy someone's garden gnomes, no one is that irrational.

The same logic does not apply to states. You cannot place a state in jail. You could do that to heads of state. But then there is such a thing called diplomatic immunity that prevents you from randomly jailing other heads of state because you might disagree with what they have done. Circling back to sovereign states as the pillar of our international society. Even the UN does not act as a real governing entity. Most resolutions are not legally binding (except from the UN Security Council but there you have the veto powers of China, the United States, France, the United Kingdom and Russia that can prevent anything harmful from happening to them or their allies). Courts only have the authority to rule if the states agree to it. And no one can force compliance with the rulings after they are made.

This all might seem disconcerting. But as you surely have noticed we do not live in total anarchy and even international relations do largely follow basic rules of our international system (at least when this book was written). To some degree, this is

---

[7] Shaw (2017), p. 1.

[8] If anarchy in the international system sounds like a strange concept, I recommend reading up on international relations theory—a few old-time international relations favorites listed here: Mearsheimer (2014) and Walt (1998).

due to the power of public international law. It creates a common set of standards that states either follow or, at a minimum, publicly claim to accept. While of course not all states are always compliant, this at least binds them to a commonly accepted set of "recognized values and standards".[9]

1.4   Who Decides What Is Public International Law?

There are four key sources of public international law. This list of four sources is not something I just invented or prioritized—it is based on Art. 38 (1) of the Statute of the International Court of Justice (ICJ).[10] Curiously, there is no equivalent of the ICJ in the wizarding world but we will get to that later. Basically, it is a court where states can resolve their conflicts. And it clearly states four key sources of public international law: (a) international conventions, (b) international custom, (c) general principles of law recognized by civilized nations and (d) judicial decisions and teachings.[11]

Art. 38 ICJ Statute

1. The Court, whose function is to decide in accordance with international law such disputes as are submitted to it, shall apply:
   a. international conventions, whether general or particular, establishing rules expressly recognized by the contesting states;
   b. international custom, as evidence of a general practice accepted as law;
   c. the general principles of law recognized by civilized nations;
   d. subject to the provisions of Article 59, judicial decisions and the teachings of the most highly qualified publicists of the various nations, as subsidiary means for the determination of rules of law

International conventions are written agreements between two or more states. They are referred to as "Conventions, International Agreements, Pacts, General Acts, Charters, through to Statutes, Declarations and Covenants".[12] A wizarding equivalent would be the International Statute of Wizarding Secrecy. There are treaties on the definition of a treaty (yes, no kidding around) that also provide insights about when treaties enter into force, to whom they apply and how to interpret them. Such wise insights can be found in the Vienna Convention on the Law of Treaties (VCLT).[13] We will skip these details here as the goal is to provide

---

[9] Shaw (2017), p. 1.

[10] Statute of the International Court of Justice of 26 June 1945, San Francisco.

[11] If you want to learn more about the different sources of public international law, here a few pointers to books that even Ms. Pince would proudly add to her collection: Shaw (2017), pp. 51 ff.; Cassese et al. (2020), pp. 181 ff.; Brierly and Clapham (2012), pp. 54 ff.

[12] Shaw (2017), p. 69.

[13] Vienna Convention on the Law of Treaties of 23 May 1969, Vienna, UNTS Vol. 1155, I-18232.

you with a first understanding of public international law, not master all details at once. Should you, however, decide to skip Advanced Potion-Making, and favor a career as lawyer over a life as an Auror, you will need to understand the intricacies of this "treaty of treaties".[14]

Customary international law requires state practice and a sense of a legal obligation (*opinio juris sive necessitates*).[15] Sounds complicated but is quite straight forward. Customary international law refers to cases in which no one has put the general agreement into a written treaty but the states believe that this rule applies and also largely act accordingly. The favorite example of legal scholars is the principle of non-refoulement. Again, sounds complicated, but is quite simple to understand: states should not send refugees or asylum seekers back to countries where they face threats to their life or freedom because of their race, religion, political opinion or other factors.[16] Yes, that seems like an obvious thing to do (for most). And by thinking that, you have understood the essence of customary international law. There are some obvious rules that might not have been written down. And that is totally fine—not every rule you follow in your private life has been codified. Some things just make sense without someone having to write it down. I'll leave it up to your own imagination to come up with moments where you behaved "correctly", but without someone having to write it down as a law. If none come to mind, this might be something else worthwhile reflecting on.

Now, there is something even more special than just pure customary international law. I am talking about *jus cogens* or peremptory norms. They enjoy "a higher rank in the international hierarchy than treaty law and even 'ordinary' customary rules"[17] as written in Art. 53 VCLT. A *jus cogens* norm needs to be accepted as customary international law and additionally be considered as non-derogable. Now what does non-derogable mean? In case of emergencies—e.g. during armed conflicts—states can suspend or suppress international law. So-called derogation clauses are for example included in International Human Rights Law (IHRL) and they allow the suspension or restriction of the exercise of certain rights. An example can be the freedom of movement. During armed conflicts, states might restrict the freedom of movement.[18] Consider for example if the death eaters had continued to stay in power and started to openly fight against the government. In this case, the government might issue a curfew at night to ensure that people are kept safe. Yes, this would restrict their freedom of movement. But it would be an emergency in which such a derogation from the human right would be legal. This is, however, not possible with

---

[14] For those of you eager to get a head start on your reading, here some initial pointers: Kolb (2016), pp. 4 ff.

[15] We now start to venture into the world of public international law, where I provide you with information on the most relevant cases and the Hermiones among you can go and read those up: ICJ, *North Sea Continental Shelf Cases (Federal Republic of Germany v. Denmark)*, Judgment, 20 February 1969, ICJ Reports 1969, § 77.

[16] More details on this principle: Kälin and Künzli (2010), p. 511.

[17] ICTY, Prosecutor v. Anto Furundzija, IT-95-17/1, Trial Judgment, 10 December 1998, para 153.

[18] ICRC (2022).

regards to all laws in question. Some laws can never be derogated from. This includes the freedom from torture and degrading treatment. For good reason. Not even a case of emergency gives the state a right to torture its citizens.

So now that we understood the different preconditions (customary international law that is non-derogable), what does this tell us about *jus cogens*? It is a special category of international law as this is what all states accept as law, in all situations. Key examples are the prohibition of the arbitrary deprivation of life,[19] torture, genocide and crimes against humanity. We will learn more about all of these categories later. But just remember, these are laws that states have to uphold and there is no talking your way out of it.[20] No single state can claim that it does not recognize a norm as *jus cogens*—there is no "persistent objector" rule.[21] Persistent objector for customary international law means the rule does not apply to you if you have always said that you disagree with it. That might work with some norms, but there is no way around *jus cogens* applying to a state. Remember this fact for when we later discuss what norms apply to wizarding states.

In many cases, lawyers have codified *jus cogens* in their international and regional treaties. Lawyers just love writing these things down, multiple times, as it gives them a feeling of adding value to a discussion if they can quote the same rule from five different sources.

Moving on to the third source of international law, let us look at **general principles of law**. To put it bluntly: if you can't find the answer you are looking for in an international treaty or in customary international law but your legal intuition tells you that no civilized nation (whatever that may be) would be ok with this, just assume that it violates a general principle of law. And then please verify. It is not always that easy. But yes, general principles fill this gap. And they are an incredibly vague concept.[22] One such example is the principle of good faith. It means that you don't enter into an agreement if you know that you are not going to keep it.

Finally, there are **judicial decisions and teachings**. They are seen as "subsidiary means for the determination of rules of law" (Art. 38 I d ICJ Statute). Wow, another one of those sentences that could have come straight from Prof. Binns and likely sends half of you back to your smartphones. Bear with me. All this means is that courts refer back to past decisions to support their ruling in a present case but they don't have to stick to a previous opinion (there is no *stare decisis* in international law, which—put in easier terms—means you can change your opinion). Similar for teachings—they are not a real source of international law but play a large role in shaping the rules that you can find in international treaties, customary international

---

[19] "Arbitrary" is included in here to leave the door open for states with the death penalty.

[20] On these norms as common non-derogable norms with *jus cogens* character: Koji (2001), p. 927. Discussing the sixteen rights considered non-derogable and named the "Paris Minimum Standards": Chowdhury (1989), pp. 147 ff.

[21] Introducing the principle of the persistent objector: Ragazzi (1997), pp. 60–62 and 67–72.

[22] Before you go into the complex legal arguments underlying this, I'd recommend that you start with this introduction: https://law.gwu.libguides.com/c.php?g=515695&p=3525705. If you are done with the intro and want to go further, you find more information on this here: Pineschi (2015).

law and general principles of law. Whether this is also the case in the wizarding world is highly questionable as the legal profession does not seem to be as mature as in the Muggle world. In addition, we can only hope that the judicial decisions don't play too big a role in shaping wizarding law given the many cases of grave miscarriage of justice (just think of Sirius and Hagrid in Azkaban).

1.5 Legal Methodology: The Equivalent of Wand Movement

Law is a lot like magical spells. It is not only what you say but how you say it. *Wingardium Leviosa* only levitates an object if you swish and flick with your wand.

Lawyers have something akin to wand movement: legal methodology. The pride of lawyers worldwide is the IRAC method: Issue, Rule, Application and Conclusion. I'll save you the time of explaining how the method works in theory and will just showcase the beauty of this structured way of arguing in the following chapters. First, I'll always raise the issue we are trying to solve. Then, we look into the rules that we need to take into consideration. We then apply the rules to the issue in question. Finally, we come to a conclusion.

Now that we have the basics covered, let's get into the specifics—the questions that have been haunting you since you opened this book.

References

ASIL (2022) Int'l law: 100 ways it shapes our lives. https://www.asil.org/resources/100Ways. Accessed 3 Dec 2022

Brierly JL, Clapham A (2012) Brierly's law of nations: an introduction to the role of international law in international relations, 7th edn. Oxford University Press, Oxford

Cassese A et al (2020) Cassese's international law, 3rd edn. Oxford University Press, Oxford

Chowdhury SR (1989) Rule of law in a state of emergency: the Paris minimum standards of human rights norms in a state of emergency. Pinter Publishers, London

ICRC (2022) Glossary. https://casebook.icrc.org/glossary/derogations. Accessed 23 June 2022

Kälin W, Künzli J (2010) The law of international human rights protection. Oxford University Press, Oxford

Koji T (2001) Emerging hierarchy in international human rights and beyond: from the perspective of non-derogable rights. Eur J Int Law 12:917–941

Kolb R (2016) The law of treaties: an introduction. Edward Elgar, Northampton

Mearsheimer J (2014) The tragedy of great power politics (Updated Edition). W. W. Norton & Company, New York

Pineschi L (2015) General principles of law – the role of the judiciary. Springer, Cham

Ragazzi M (1997) The concept of international obligations erga omnes. Clarendon Press, Oxford

Rowling JK (1997) Harry Potter and the philosopher's stone. Bloomsbury, London

Shaw MN (2017) International law, 8th edn. Cambridge University Press, Cambridge

Torremans P, Fawcett JJ, Grušić U (2017) Cheshire, North & Fawcett private international law, 15th edn. Oxford University Press, Oxford

Walt SM (1998) International relations: one world, many theories. Foreign Policy 110

Public International Law

2

Abstract

This chapter explains the basics of public international law, starting with how we define a state. Based on this understanding, we will assess whether there are wizarding states or not. Next, the concept of state responsibility is applied to crimes of witches and wizards. We also dive deeper into the concept of jurisdiction to understand who has to lead criminal cases against witches and wizards when they are violating the law (and who gets to figure out how to keep someone with magical powers locked up in a cell). We also look into enforcement of international law and apply this to the wizarding world. Finally, this chapter gives an overview of immunity and how it works across the different worlds.

2.1   Are There Wizarding States?

The first and very fundamental question we want to address is: are there wizarding states? This might seem random, but the background of the question is clear. We need to understand whether wizarding communities are considered a state and can thus be subject to public international law. For this, wizarding communities in the different Muggle countries would need to be considered a state. So, let's start applying the IRAC methodology to solve these questions.

2.1.1   Elements of a State

As we lack knowledge of the wizarding world's legal system and theory on public international law, we first must look at the way in which we define states. Based on long-established theories by lawyers, a state requires a permanent population,

© The Author(s), under exclusive license to Springer Nature Switzerland AG 2024   9
F. Heidemann, *An International Law Perspective on Harry Potter*,
Springer Textbooks in Law, https://doi.org/10.1007/978-3-031-57571-6_2

defined territory and a government.[1] These are the fundamental elements of sovereign states. The state further needs to have the capacity to enter into relations with other states.[2] This all sounds very abstract, so let's break it down into smaller pieces.

First, you need a **permanent population**. But what is permanent? It doesn't mean that you always need to have the same number of people considered as your population. It rather refers to the way in which the population lives, meaning it differentiates populations that are permanently living within a territory from nomadic populations. There is no minimum number of inhabitants required to fulfill the permanent population requirement. Otherwise, small island nations like Tuvalu with only about 12,000 inhabitants could never be considered a state.[3]

Second, you need a **defined territory**. This does not mean, that the territorial boundaries have to be undisputed. There only needs to be "a band of territory which is undeniably controlled by the government of the alleged state".[4] The territory of the state can be split into distinct parts, all that is required is a "stable community within a certain area".[5]

Third, you need some **form of government**. There are debates about the political structures required.[6] The threshold is however not very high. Even if a state is in the midst of a civil war or other conflict and only exercises control over parts of its territory, it can be considered an independent country. In these cases, the state does not cease to exist. As a rule of thumb, it is possible that a "new" state gets recognized as independent even if it lacks control over its entire territory. In these situations, the state does however need to balance the lack of control with significant international recognition.[7]

Law would not require lawyers if this were all there is to the story. In addition to these three elements, states also need to be able to **enter into relations with other states**. The state therefore needs to be independent.[8] This criterion is the most tricky one and heavily disputed. There will always be political disputes about whether or not a country is recognized and can enter into relations with others. But political dynamics aside, the fact that the state could enter into relations with others and does so with at least some states should be seen as sufficient here.[9]

---

[1] See: Shaw (2017), p. 157.

[2] These criteria are among others laid down in Art. 1 of the Montevideo Convention on Rights and Duties of the State: 165 League of Nations Treaty Series 19; Shaw (2017), p. 157.

[3] Shaw (2017), p. 158. More on the tiny island of Tuvalu: CIA World Factbook (2022).

[4] Shaw (2017), p. 157.

[5] ibid., pp. 158–159. (Btw: ibid. is just a clever looking way of saying "look at the previous footnote, I'm too lazy to spell it out again).

[6] ibid., p. 159.

[7] ibid., p. 160.

[8] Elaborating on the different cases in which the capacity to enter into relations with other states was in question: ibid., pp. 160–161.

[9] For a fascinating example of the complexities of law and the way in which people try to establish new states, refer to the fascinating example of Sealand, a platform in the North Sea which a former

Taking these key elements of states into consideration, we now must look at the wizarding world to assess whether states exist among wizards as well. This means we must apply the rules to the issue in question to understand whether there are wizarding states.

2.1.2 Do Wizards Have a Permanent Population?

The first key question is: how many wizards are there? Given the secrecy of the wizarding community, there are no reliable facts on this. Yet, for Britain there is a reliable estimate of about 3000 witches and wizards.[10] Interestingly, up to 33% of the wizarding population is made up of children between the age of 11–18, given that Hogwarts has a capacity of 1000 students yet Britain as such only has about 3000 witches and wizards. One reason could be the violent years under Voldemort. There might however be other explanations, such as a high enrollment of foreign students (though not specifically mentioned), a student body which is not living up to the capacity of the wizarding school or surprisingly high birth rates among Muggle-born[11] witches and wizards, migration of grown-up witches and wizards from the UK to other wizarding countries.[12]

The fact that there are thirteen Quidditch Teams in Britain and Ireland[13] also speaks to a possibly higher number of witches and wizards living in the country. Each team requires at least seven players (making it a total of 91 players). As only a few of Harry's classmates end up playing in one of the teams, this would indicate that the wizarding population is indeed larger.

Leaving those debates about the demographics within the wizarding community aside, let us return to the question whether the population requirement is fulfilled. The Pacific Island nation Niue is considered a state with a population of only about 1900.[14] The population size of the wizarding world is therefore sufficient to fulfill this criterion of statehood, even if we follow the lower estimate of only 2000 inhabitants.

> **The Mystery of Dual Citizenship**
> Another valid question any Potterhead will likely contemplate: are the witches and wizards really nationals of the wizarding state or nationals of their

(continued)

---

pirate radio broadcaster had occupied in the 1960s and where he had declared the sovereign Principality of Sealand: Grimmelmann (2012), pp. 405–484; Shaw (2017), p. 162.

[10] J. K. Rowling made this estimate in the "MuggleNet and Leaky Cauldron Interview" (2005b).

[11] Referred to as non-magical or "no-maj" in the United States (U.S.).

[12] Further elaborating on this fascinating issue: Wellingtongoose (2015).

[13] Rowling and Whisp (n.d.), p. 63.

[14] More on one of the world's smallest countries: CIA World Factbook, Niue.

respective Muggle nation? Consider for example Hermione Granger, who is Muggle-born and didn't know about her magical abilities until she received her letter from Hogwarts. She is certainly a British citizen, at least until she enters the wizarding world. But does it change then? We simply don't know. There also is no clarity on whether attendance of Hogwarts is considered as fulfilling the wizarding world's nationality requirement. But we must assume that wizards and Muggles have found a way of dealing with this phenomenon, in particular with regards to Muggle-born wizards and witches. For the purpose of this book, we'll therefore assume that all witches and wizards are either only nationals of their wizarding state or hold dual citizenship. This question does thereby not have an impact on the question of whether there is a sufficient number of witches and wizards.

2.1.3   Is the Wizarding Territory Fixed?

The wizarding world is the magical community, a society in which wizards and witches live. Much of the wizarding world is hidden from Muggle eyes. To examine whether the wizarding territory fulfills the requirements under international law, we'll again take the wizarding community of Great Britain as an example. The reason for this is simple: the documentation of the wizarding communities in Great Britain and the United States is far better than any information available on other wizarding communities. As scarce data is a researcher's curse, we'll make our life as simple as possible and rely on those cases for the assessments.[15]

The wizarding territory in Great Britain does not compare to Muggle states as it consists of several locations spread across the territory of a Muggle nation. While connected in ways unfathomable to most of us (just think about stepping into your chimney), the locations are more interconnected than enclaves. And even enclaves can be part of a state. Hogsmeade as such can be considered sufficiently "fixed" to fulfill the territorial criterion of statehood. With this given, there is no reason to assume that the other locations cannot also be part of this wizard state. After all, rules have to be interpreted also taking into account the circumstances of the case in question. As for this case, the special connectedness of the territory allows for the conclusion that there indeed is a wizard state. The only remaining question is whether it is problematic that the government institutions are not located in Hogsmeade but in London. There is no provision under international law stating that government institutions of a state have to be located in the largest fixed territory. Instead, it is possible that government institutions would be in an enclave. We will

---

[15] Please take this as an encouragement for a more thorough study of the wizarding world in Africa and Asia.

therefore assume that the fact that the Ministry of Magic is located in London is not problematic.

2.1.4   Do Wizards Have a Government?

Let's make this quick: absolutely. The British Ministry of Magic was formally established in 1707.[16] Prior to its founding, the Wizard's Council was the longest serving body governing the British magical community.[17] Yet, after the International Statute of Secrecy was imposed in 1692, the wizarding community required a more structured, organized, and complex governing system to support, regulate and communicate with the newly hidden wizarding community.[18] In general, the Minister of Magic is democratically elected, although there were cases during times of crisis in which the position was offered to individuals without a public vote.[19] Ministers of Magic must hold regular elections at least every 7 years, although there is no fixed term limit. The average time in office for Ministers of Magic would however leave Italian Prime Ministers envious.[20]

While Ministry of Magic might sound confusing (given that other governments label specific departments as "Ministry" while referring to the entire organization as "British government") this distinction will be excused, especially as the set-up of the Ministry indicates that it indeed covers the entirety of wizarding affairs. To explain, within the British Ministry of Magic, there are seven main departments: the departments of Magical Law Enforcement, Magical Accidents and Catastrophes, Magical Transportation, Mysteries, Magical Games and Sports, Regulation and Control of Magical Creatures, and International Magical Cooperation.

The Minister of Magic has sole jurisdiction over his Ministry. There are, however, emergency visits to the Muggle Prime Minister by the Minister of Magic. These visits are announced by a portrait of the first Minister for Magic, Ulick Gamp, that hangs in the Muggle Prime Minister's study in 10 Downing Street.[21] One such example were the horrible events associated with the return of Voldemort, when previous Minister for Magic Cornelius Fudge and later his successor Rufus Scrimgeour visited the UK Prime Minister in his office.[22]

---

[16] Rowling (2015), Ministers for Magic.

[17] Rowling (2015), Ministers for Magic.

[18] Rowling (2015), Ministers for Magic.

[19] The offer was for example made to Albus Dumbledore, who repeatedly turned it down. More in: Rowling (2015), Ministers for Magic.

[20] ibid.

[21] ibid.

[22] Rowling (2005a), Chapter 1: The Other Minister.

2.1.5   Are There Relations Between Different Wizarding States?

Yes, wizarding governments even have departments in the ministry dedicated to this. Even prior to this, for example the Native American magical community and those in Europe as well as Africa knew about one another, being aware of the similarities between their communities.[23]

Between the Ministries of Magic in the respective wizarding countries, there are established means of cooperation. The British Ministry of Magic for example has a special Department for this purpose. Within the British Department of International Magical Cooperation, there are three Divisions: the International Confederation of Wizards, the International Magical Office of Law and the International Magical Trading Standards Body. There is thus a complex network of agreements between different states which enables and regulates cooperation.

2.1.6   Recognition of the Wizarding States

States aim to be recognized by other states to legitimize their sovereignty. Because of the International Statute of Secrecy of 1692, it can be argued that the wizarding states never intended to be recognized by other sovereign states (which were then only starting to emerge).[24] Yet, the International Statute of Secrecy only concerns the relations between the Muggle world and wizards. Between wizarding states, however, there has been exchange and a sufficient level of recognition.

Between the Muggle world and the wizarding world, the exchange depends on the country in question. As already mentioned, there was information exchange in Britain. In the U.S., however, a breach of the International Statute of Secrecy led to Rappaport's law, which enforced strict segregation between the Muggles (called No-Majs) and wizarding communities.

2.1.7   Yes, Wizards Live in Their Own States, of Sorts

Our look at wizarding populations, territory and governments has shown that the wizarding state of Britain fulfills the criteria of a state. It is a tiny state, indeed. With an even tinier fixed territory. But the fact that the wizarding world functions differently because of, well, magic, also allows for a small deviation from the strict requirement of a fixed territory. If Hogsmeade suffices as a fixed territory and the other locations are linked to this territory like enclaves fulfills the most critical criterion. In addition, the wizarding states recognize each other (e.g., the wizarding state of Britain and that of the U.S.). So, yes, witches and wizards live in their own states. They have their own legal regimes, upheld by the Ministry of Magic. This

---

[23]More on wizards in North America in: Rowling (2016), Seventeenth Century and Beyond.

[24]The International Statute of Secrecy was signed in 1689 and entered into force in 1692.

understanding does, however, lead to a bunch of follow-up questions ranging from jurisdiction to responsibility for crimes of witches and wizards.

2.2   When Is a Wizarding State Responsible for the Crimes of Wizards?

2.2.1   State Responsibility

Lawyers have set up complicated legal rules to assess when a state is responsible for the acts of its citizens. Yes, states are not responsible for all of the acts of all their citizens both inside and outside of the country all the time. Imagine what chaos that would lead to. If Dudley and his gang would decide to beat up an innocent child from the neighborhood and the British government would be held fully responsible. The only solution would be to have some member of the British government tail Dudley and his gang of insecure bullies at all times and thereby ensure that no harm is done. Great idea, but not feasible given the range and number of bullying youngsters.

So instead of assuming that a government is responsible for every single act of its citizens, there have to be boundaries. These boundaries have been laid out in the Articles on State Responsibility (ASR) by the International Law Commission (ILC). The ASR were adopted by the ILC in 2001 and have found their way into numerous judgments of international courts and tribunals.[25] They are largely considered customary international law.[26] As we now all know, customary international law is a source of international law and will offer us some answers to the question of when a state is responsible for the acts of its citizens and—taking it one step further—in which cases is a wizarding state responsible for the acts of witches and wizards. As the wizarding state would also have to uphold customary international law, we can assume that the ASR apply to it as well.

Art. 1 ASR

Every internationally wrongful act of a State entails the international responsibility of that State.

The general rule sounds quite simple and is laid out in Art. 1 ASR: "Every internationally wrongful act of a State entails the international responsibility of that State." So far, so good. But what do we make of this? Art. 2 ASR helps us with this.

---

[25] ILC (2001) (in the following, I'll refer to this as ASR Commentary).

[26] UN Legislative Series, Book 25: *Materials on the Responsibility of States for Internationally Wrongful Acts,* 2012, UN Doc. ST/LEG/SER.B/25 viii. For those who are eager to learn more about the ASR and the codification process, I am making use of shameless self-promotion and can refer you to this excellent book: Renz (2020), pp. 46ff. Excellent book. And yes, there was a change in last name. You can find my writing listed under Renz. For future books look for Heidemann.

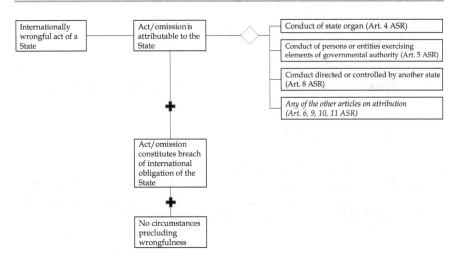

Fig. 2.1 State responsibility

Art. 2 ASR

There is an internationally wrongful act of a State when conduct consisting of an action or omission (a) is attributable to the State under international law; and (b) constitutes a breach of an international obligation of the State

Now, lucky for you I always sympathized with Hermione for wanting to read the next few chapters in the text book and I can tell you that there is much more to these rules, including certain circumstances that ensure that states are not held responsible, even if an act was attributable and if it constitutes a breach of its international legal obligations. We'll also add this to our check list of when states can be held accountable for acts of their citizens. To avoid that we jump directly into complicated detailed debates, let us first take a look at the overall rules on attribution, breach and circumstances precluding wrongfulness to understand the basics. There will be specific examples on different cases to assess whether the rules would be applicable (Fig. 2.1).

2.2.2   When Are Acts Attributable to a State?

As mentioned earlier, not every act by anyone can be attributed to a state. But what does attribution mean? The dictionary definition of attribution is to regard something as being caused by a person or thing.[27] In real life, this could be something along the following example: I hear a loud bang in the living room, walk over and see my cat

---

[27] Cambridge Dictionary (2022).

close to grandma's beautiful broken vase on the floor, chances are high that I'll attribute the damage to the cat. Especially if the cat is called Crookshanks and I'm not a cat person.

In the context of state responsibility the question is if you can link the breach of an international legal obligation to the state. You can only do this in very specific situations, which have—lucky for us—been elaborated in the ASR. There is a wide range of different scenarios for attribution: conduct of state organs (Art. 4 ASR), conduct of persons or entities exercising elements of governmental authority (Art. 5 ASR), conduct of organs placed at the disposal of a state by another state (Art. 6 ASR), conduct directed or controlled by a state (Art. 8 ASR), conduct carried out in the absence or default of the official authority (Art. 9 ASR), conduct of an insurrectional or other movement (Art. 10 ASR) and—finally—conduct acknowledged and adopted by a state as its own (Art. 11 ASR). Yes, I agree, this list is long. Unsurprisingly, not all of those are equally relevant and we will focus on the most important options for attribution: Art. 4, Art. 5 and Art. 8 ASR. With this, you'll have the majority of cases covered. And for everything else there are plenty of more books out there for you to go deeper into these questions.[28]

2.2.2.1 Who Is Considered a State Organ: Fudge vs. Percy?

Art. 4 ASR

1. The conduct of any State organ shall be considered an act of that State under international law, whether the organ exercises legislative, executive, judicial or any other functions, whatever position it holds in the organization of the State, and whatever its character as an organ of the central Government or of a territorial unit of the State.
2. An organ includes any person or entity which has that status in accordance with the internal law of the State.

A state organ is "every person or entity which has that status in accordance with the internal law" (Art. 4 ASR). Great, now please explain to me what this means in plain English. Simply put: every person who works for the government (both civil servants and political appointees), no matter in which position, whether for a regional or a state government, even the Prime Minister themself.[29]

---

[28] Crawford et al. (2010).

[29] Additional discussion on this can be found in Momtaz (2010), pp. 239–242. In general on this: ASR Commentary, Art. 4, N 5-9. More on attribution of legislative organs: Permanent Court of International Justice (PCIJ) (interestingly enough, the PCIJ was not so permanent after all, only existing from 1922 to 1946, its successor is the ICJ), *German Settlers in Poland*, Advisory Opinion, 10 September 1923, PCIJ Series B No. 6, pp. 35–36; PCIJ, *Treatment of Polish Nationals and Other Persons of Polish Origin or Speech in the Danzig Region*, Advisory Opinion, 4 February 1932, PCIJ Series A/B No. 44, pp. 24–25; PCIJ, *Phosphates in Morocco Kingdom of Italy v. French Republic)*, Judgment, 14 June 1938, PCIJ Series A/B No. 74, p. 25; ICJ, *Rights of Nationals of the United States of America in Morocco (France v. United States of America)*, Judgment, 27 August

Let's take Percy Weasley as an example, he is the ideal person to envision what being a state organ means (and yes, I know the word is weird, but state organ can just mean an individual—just try not to go too visual on the organ metaphor), as pretty much anything he does is linked to his work for the Ministry of Magic. But while it is evident that his acts are linked to the wizarding state if it concerns cauldron size, what about private disputes he might have with this family? What if he had actually fought his parents because they refused to fall in line with Fudge's policy decision to mistrust Harry and Dumbledore? Here comes the decision between acts in an "official capacity" and those in a purely "private capacity". If Percy had fought his parents on Fudge's orders, his acts would have been attributable to the wizarding state. If he had done so as part of him just being a lousy son, this would have been his private capacity. In that case, the wizarding state would not be considered responsible. Lucky for the lawyers among us, Percy Weasley is one of those making this distinction very easy as he is almost never acting in a private capacity).[30]

If we look at other cases, a clear example for attributable behavior given the role as state organ are the acts of Minister for Magic, Cornelius Fudge. In this role, anything he does in official capacity is considered an act of the state. But what if he goes beyond his official mandate, while still acting in an official capacity? Let's assume the Wizengamot (essentially the wizarding world's high court) had told him to come to his senses and accept the reality of Voldemort's return but he had continued to act as though that had not happened. Contravening instructions or exceeding one's authority while still acting in the official capacity as a state organ is no excuse for the state. This is lovingly called an *ultra vires* act and the acts would still be attributable to the state.

A more complicated case is Minister for Magic, Pius Thicknesse. During his term, he was under the *Imperius* curse and thus unable to exercise his free will. In his role though, he is still considered a state organ. The question of the *Imperius* curse will be more relevant regarding the circumstances precluding wrongfulness. But yes, whether Fudge, Thicknesse or Percy Weasley, all of them can be considered state organs and their acts—while in official capacity—can be attributed to the wizarding state based on Art. 4 ASR.

Now, if we make matters a bit more complicated, how about the acts of Voldemort? If we take a look at the state organ definition, the initial reaction would be: Of course not, he has no official role in the wizarding government. This instinct is fully correct when we discuss *de jure* state organs, meaning those, who are legally considered state organs. The situation might be different if we widen our assessment to also include *de facto* state organs.

The term "state organ" can be interpreted more widely under public international law. It has become an accepted reality that private individuals or entities can achieve

---

1952, ICJ Reports 1952, pp. 193–194. Cases regarding judicial organs: ICJ, *Difference Relating to Immunity from Legal Process of a Special Rapporteur of the Commission on Human Rights,* Advisory Opinion, 29 April 1999, ICJ Reports, §§ 62–63.

[30] For more on this fun exchange, refer to: Rowling (2007), Chapter 31: The Battle of Hogwarts.

a status equivalent to that of the *de jure* organs. The goal is to prevent states from avoiding responsibility by denying organ status to certain entities.[31] Just assume a state asks a private group (e.g., the equivalent of retired death eaters) to conduct crimes on its behalf (e.g., getting rid of political opponents). When the crimes become known, the state just highlights that this group's members were not state organs. Seems unfair, doesn't it. This is what the concept of *de jure* organs tries to prevent. The critical test is whether the person or entity is "completely dependent" upon the state. Now try to think about Voldemort as completely dependent and then try not to laugh out loud. Yes, exactly. Does not seem like a good case for it, but still, worth the thought. So while we will assess how we can make sure that Voldemort answers for the crimes he committed, it will be tricky to pin them to the wizarding state based on Art. 4 ASR.

2.2.2.2 Do the Dementors Exercise Elements of Governmental Authority?

Art. 5 ASR

The conduct of a person or entity which is not an organ of the State under article 4 but which is empowered by the law of that State to exercise elements of the governmental authority shall be considered an act of the State under international law, provided the person or entity is action in that capacity in the particular instance.

Elements of governmental authority is another one of those tricky terms. This is an acknowledgement that non-state entities are increasingly playing roles that were previously considered purely tasks of the government (if you want to impress your lawyer friends, refer to those as *acta jure imperii*). If we want to understand whether the dementors were exercising elements of governmental authority in their role as guards of Azkaban, we have to understand the two elements of Art. 5 ASR: "empowered by the law" and "governmental authority".

Empowerment by the law can be interpreted in different ways. Yes, as you will have noted by now, there are many grey areas in law and many different ways to interpret the exact same sentence or even word. If you look at the narrow interpretation, a specific law has to be issued to grant governmental powers to the person or entity. We can quickly discard that. At least based on official records we have received from the wizarding world, it is highly unlikely that there is such a thing as a law granting the dementors powers. So let's move on to the wider definition. Based on that, a government agency needs to be empowered under internal law to delegate the role—in this case guarding Azkaban—to the person or entity. We unfortunately don't have any insights into the laws underlying the wizarding prison

---

[31] Condorelli and Kress (2010), p. 230.

Azkaban. Yet, even if there were a law that empowered a government agency to delegate the role of guarding Azkaban to another person or entity—could that apply here? This leads us to a fascinating question: can the dementors be considered a person or entity? Well, they are a scary bunch. Certainly not a person, at least if you believe in the best in humanity. But an entity? Interesting thought, isn't it? The ASR Commentary describes "entity" as "public corporations, semi-public entities, public agencies of various kinds and even, in special cases, private companies".[32] Now to be fair, none of these sound like a good description for the dementors. So even if there would have been proper laws in place to empower the delegation of the guarding of Azkaban to a third party, the dementors will not fit the description of what the lawmakers had in mind.

As for the other test on "governmental authority"—this would have been a direct fit given that guarding prisoners is considered as one of the typical examples for governmental authority.[33] So let's bear that in mind when the wizarding community decides to instate some real person or entity as guard for Azkaban (yes, the dementors no longer guard Azkaban, Kingsley Shacklebolt made sure of that—the guards are now Aurors, who clearly fall under Art. 4 ASR as they are state organs).[34]

So no, there will be no attribution of the dementors' acts based on Art. 5 ASR. That does, however, not mean that the wizarding community is off the hook for letting dementors roam around the wizarding prison for centuries (one of the early cost saving measures of the ministry, based on Minister of Magic Damocles Rowle). Instead, we'll have to look at ways to hold the ministry employees themselves accountable for this. More on that to follow when we look at the definition of torture.[35]

2.2.2.3 Are the Death Eaters Controlled by the State?

Art. 8 ASR

The conduct of a person or group of persons shall be considered an act of a State under international law if the person or group of persons is in fact acting on the instructions of, or under direction or control of, that State in carrying out the conduct.

When hearing about the many horrible crimes committed by the death eaters after Voldemort's return—just think about them killing people for fun—did you also wonder whether the wizarding state should be held accountable for it? Before we can assess if the state could bring the wizarding state to court, we have to understand if

---

[32] ASR Commentary, Art. 5, p. 43.

[33] ibid.

[34] If this is news to you, you will need to read up here: Rowling (2015).

[35] For more on this please go to Sect. 4.5.

the acts of the death eaters can be attributed to the state. Most of the death eaters are not state organs and certainly not acting in an official capacity when they go about killing people. There will also not be an explicit empowerment by the law that would lead to attribution under Art. 5 ASR. This leaves us with the test of Art. 8 ASR.

There are three options for attribution to the State under Art. 8 ASR: instruction, direction and control. Let's have a quick look at all three of them before assessing what might apply to the death eaters. Instruction means a state decides to perform a certain task and then instructs a non-state entity to carry it out.[36] Classic "I know what I want but would prefer to not get my hands dirty". The second option is direction, in which the entity is subordinate to the state and the state shows the entity how to conduct the operation. The last option is also the most tricky one: control.[37] There are several differing legal judgments linked to the question what control means in the context of Art. 8 ASR.[38] Important to remember is that we have to apply a so-called "effective control" test based on the ICJ judgment in the *Nicaragua* and *Genocide* case (tell that to any lawyer and they'll be super impressed).[39] In the *Nicaragua* case, the ICJ stated that the state needs to determine the beginning of the activities, the means by which they are implemented and the end of the acts.[40] It is not sufficient to just provide financial support, help the entity organize, train them or supply them with equipment.

Let's just think about what this might mean for the death eaters before sending you off for a quick butter beer break to digest all this new information. When the death eaters go around killing people, attacking Hogwarts or locking up students and goblins in basements, they would have to be instructed, directed or controlled by the wizarding state to lead to state responsibility under Art. 8 ASR. We don't know of any direct instruction or direction, that could support this argument. The only option left is therefore control by the state. But even that seems highly unlikely if you think in more detail about the time after Voldemort's return. Initially, the Ministry of Magic actively ignored that the death eaters were roaming around. Afterwards, when Pius Thicknesse had taken over the Ministry while under the *Imperius* curse, he supported the work of Voldemort but did not—at least to our knowledge—control their activities. Quite the opposite, they were controlling him. So no, we won't be able to hold the wizarding state responsible for the acts of the group of death eaters

---

[36] On attribution based on instruction refer to: Renz (2020), pp. 137 ff. Additionally, check out: ASR Commentary, Art. 8, pp. 47 ff.

[37] More on those different options: ASR Commentary, Art. 8, pp. 47 ff.

[38] I'll send you to more detailed books and articles if you want to follow-up on all the differences: Renz (2020), pp. 137 ff.; Mačák (2016), pp. 411 ff.; Cassese (2007), p. 663; Kolb (2017), pp. 80ff.

[39] On these tests: Renz (2020), pp. 141 ff.

[40] On the Nicaragua case and the effective control test: ICJ, *Military and Paramilitary Activities in and against Nicaragua (Nicaragua v. United States of America)*, Judgment, 27 June 1986, ICJ Reports 1986, § 115; Renz (2020), pp. 141 ff. On the Genocide case: ICJ, *Application of the Convention on the Prevention and Punishment of the Crime of Genocide (Bosnia and Herzegovina v. Serbia and Montenegro)*, Judgment, 26 February 2007, ICJ Reports 2007, §§ 402–406.

based on Art. 8 ASR. But there is much more to look into, so don't despair, we'll get around to how to hold the wizarding state responsible.

2.2.3   Breach of International Legal Obligations vs. Bad Politics

Art. 12 ASR

There is a breach of an international obligation by a State when an act of that State is not in conformity with what is required of it by that obligation, regardless of its origin or character.

As mentioned at the beginning of this chapter, it is an internationally wrongful act of a state when an act or omission can be (1) attributed to the state and (2) constitutes a breach of an international legal obligation (Art. 2 ASR). When we talk about a breach of an international legal obligation, it is important to distinguish between a real breach and just bad politics. Bad politics is harmful in its own way, but does not equal a breach of an international obligation. One such example is when Fudge ignored the return of Voldemort after the Triwizard Tournament incident, enabling the death eaters and Voldemort to organize and gain strength, while the Ministry focused on Dumbledore as enemy number one. Stupidity is, unfortunately, not a crime under international law.

So let's look deeper into the concept of breach of international legal obligations. It depends on the state in question what is considered a breach of international law as states have committed to different laws multilaterally, bilaterally as well as unilaterally (in simple terms—they committed to uphold the rules as part of a large group, in a relationship to one other state or just by themselves).[41] We can't just hold all states accountable to the same rules as (and now we circle back to the beginning of this book) states are considered sovereign and have to decide by themselves which rules they want to abide by. There are some exceptions that are applicable to all states as the Hermione's among you will remember: these rules are considered *jus cogens*.[42] But aside from those rules it depends on the state in question. We will therefore have to look at each state and assess what they committed to as part of international treaties, customary international law or unilateral obligations.

For the wizarding world, there is limited expectation that they have actively signed any treaties of Muggle international law. So the only rules that will for sure apply to them are those of *jus cogens* as they apply to all states, regardless of whether they want them to.

For those rules, it is important for the wizarding world to note that they always create positive as well as negative obligations. To take a simple example: the *jus*

---

[41] More on those different types of obligations: Renz (2020), pp. 71–79.

[42] For all the non-Hermiones here, please jump back to Sect. 1.4.

cogens norm that forbids torture. States have to refrain from torturing anyone (negative obligation = don't torture) and they also have to do their best to prevent torture from occurring (positive obligation = stop others from torturing as far as you can). States can therefore breach their international legal obligations both if the state acts in the wrong way (meaning it tortures its citizens) or if it fails to act (meaning it actively ignores a problem and does not take all necessary steps).

So to take this back to an example of the wizarding world: once the death eaters are killing Muggles as well as fellow witches and wizards, the Ministry of Magic would have the obligation to prevent the killing and would need to do whatever it can reasonably do to stop them. Of course, there is no expectation that every killing or every violent act can be prevented by the state. But the Ministry at least has to exercise due diligence. This means in lawyerly language that if the State "knew or must have known of the real and immediate risk" and it "failed to exercise the required standard of care", this will be considered a violation of its due diligence.[43]

Looking at another example, let's assess the situation after the Battle of the Department of Mysteries, when everyone had started to realize that Voldemort indeed returned. The Ministry knew that many people were starting to sell fake protective spells and charmed objects. Now when assessing whether the Ministry of Magic was living up to its due diligence obligations to prevent people from being harmed by this, we have to apply the due diligence test that it "knew or must have known of the real and immediate risk"—as described the Ministry knew so that part is given. To lead to state responsibility, it must have "failed to exercise the required standard of care". The Ministry of Magic set up the Office for the Detection and Confiscation of Counterfeit Defensive Spells and Protective Objects, headed by Arthur Weasley. The Office was charged with confiscating these objects and ensure that they did not harm the wizarding population.[44] Now while one might argue if this was the most effective measure, we can't dispute that the Ministry reacted to protect its population. There was therefore no violation of the due diligence obligations in this case.

2.2.4 Circumstances Precluding Wrongfulness: I.e. the Dragon Ate My Homework

The ASR offer several circumstances precluding wrongfulness. All this means is that if the situation applies, the state's act will not be considered wrongful, even if it violated international legal obligations. It is—to make it sound less complicated— the list of excuses that gets you out of trouble. Similar to if you didn't do your homework and had to provide a convincing excuse. Well, at least in some classes such as with Prof. Flitwick it would probably have helped. For states, the list of

---

[43] More on the due diligence principle in: Renz (2020), pp. 85–89.

[44] Rowling (2005a), Chapter 5: An Excess of Phlegm.

excuses does not cover the dragon eating your homework or the troll entering the dungeon and you not having access to your books.

States have to come up with something more convincing. If states breach international legal obligations, there are only some circumstances that preclude the wrongfulness of their action: (1) consent, (2) self-defense, (3) countermeasure, (4) force majeure, (5) distress and (6) necessity. I will leave a detailed explanation of these circumstances precluding wrongfulness for others to cover, but just beware that they exist and they might mean that a state cannot be held responsible.[45]

2.3 Who Has Jurisdiction over Crimes Committed by Wizards?

2.3.1 What Is Jurisdiction?

Now that we explained that there are cases in which states have to answer for their behavior (and we'll learn later that this also holds true for individuals), another important concept to tackle concerns the ability of a state to judge a certain case. This concerns the topic of jurisdiction. Jurisdiction is one of those terms lawyers love. If there is limited content to fight over at court or you know that you'll lose the arguments based on the legal merits, you can always discuss that the court did not have jurisdiction to decide over the case (of course, this is also sometimes a legitimate argument). But what does jurisdiction really mean? Let's ask a lawyer. As Shaw (one of those you should remember) states: "Jurisdiction concerns the power of the state under international law to regulate or otherwise impact upon people, property and circumstances and reflects the basic principles of state sovereignty, equality of states and non-interference in domestic affairs."[46] Heavy stuff. Let's break it down by looking at how it applies to the wizarding world.

2.3.2 What Does Jurisdiction Mean for Wizards?

How do you explain jurisdiction to witches and wizards who didn't go through law schools? Quite simply: if you're a witch or a wizard and you break something or injure someone, do you have to go before a regular court or will you end up in Azkaban? That is what jurisdiction is all about. In general, one needs to distinguish between civil and criminal jurisdiction. Civil law concerns cases such as when someone from Germany violates the terms of a contract he or she signed with a someone from France. In those cases, you need to know whether to go before a German or French court. Given the limited economic interaction between Muggles

---

[45]More on the circumstances precluding wrongfulness: Kolb (2017), pp. 109 ff.; Shaw (2017), pp. 601 ff.
[46]Shaw (2017), pp. 645 ff.

and wizards, we will leave this question aside.[47] Criminal jurisdiction is significantly more relevant. This concerns cases in which the citizen of one country violates criminal law in another country. Where will they have to answer before court? Translating this into interactions with the wizarding world is even more complicated.

Think back to all the crimes committed by death eaters. Will they have to go to a regular courts? Would this even be possible? Without dementors, who would ensure that they not just *Alohomora* their way out of prison? For these reasons, let's take a deeper look at jurisdiction between the wizarding and Muggle world in cases concerning criminal law. Criminal jurisdiction distinguishes between three key principles: the territorial principle, the nationality principle and the passive personality principle.[48]

2.3.3 What Is the Territorial Principle?

Under the territorial principle, states can prosecute crimes which were committed within their borders. There are a few more complicated regulations such as crimes committed on airplanes, in the air space above a country and on vessels. But let's leave those aside and focus on the essentials. You commit a crime in another country, you're better prepared to stand trial in that country (let's also ignore the many intricacies that come with phenomena such as private military and security contractors operating in conflict zones and avoiding foreign jurisdiction and pretend to be in a picture-perfect world, where the territorial principle actually functions).[49]

2.3.4 What Does the Nationality Principle Mean?

The nationality principle allows a state to exercise criminal jurisdiction (meaning to hold a trial against) its nationals even if they committed crimes in another country.[50] This is, however, usually limited to very severe cases. E.g., the UK limits the exercise of jurisdiction based on the nationality principles to acts such as treason, murder and bigamy committed by its citizens abroad. Imagine other scenarios, in which the UK courts would have to hold a hearing for every case in which a crime was committed by a UK citizen overseas. They would simply not have time for other issues such as discussions about rightful parliamentary practices during Brexit.[51]

---

[47] Although the question is quite fascinating when you think about what happens if a wizard buys furniture in a Muggle store and wants to reclaim VAT when entering Hogsmeade.

[48] Shaw (2017), pp. 488 ff.

[49] ibid., pp. 488–493. More on the underlying principle of territorial sovereignty regarding criminal acts in the *Lotus* case: PCIJ, Series A, No. 10, 1927. More on these discussions in Renz (2020).

[50] Shaw (2017), pp. 493–497.

[51] For those of you who know what BeReal is but who missed out on the entire Brexit discussions, Google it, trust me, there is plenty to read up on.

2.3.5   Let's Talk About Passive Personality

The passive personality principle sounds most complicated but simply means that if someone commits a crime against a national from your state, your state can prosecute this person even if the crime was committed abroad. So, if a Brit is hurt by an Italian, the British state can charge the Italian citizen for the crime.[52]

2.3.6   How Do We Choose Between Different States with Jurisdiction?

If these technical terms haven't petrified you yet, you might have asked if this cannot lead to situations in which several states would be able to prosecute the criminal. Yes, indeed. That is the case. And that is why there will need to be discussions between the states regarding who has the right to exercise jurisdiction in the specific case.[53] But instead of taking a deep dive into those discussions about jurisdiction, let's see whether this is necessary in the context of debates between the wizarding and Muggle legal communities.

2.3.7   So, Who Has Jurisdiction, Regular Courts or the Wizengamot?

When looking at examples from the British wizarding world, there indeed appear to be agreements between Muggles and wizards as to who has jurisdiction over crimes committed by wizards. A clear example is the warning about the escaped prisoner Sirius Black, which is issued on TV even though there is no information provided on where he fled from.[54] It is later clarified that the Minister of Magic, Cornelius Fudge, informed the Muggle Prime Minister of Black's escape from Azkaban fortress. Black had supposedly killed twelve Muggles but was still charged under wizarding jurisdiction and the Muggle Prime Minister was obviously aware of this.[55] Therefore, jurisdiction for crimes by wizards, even if committed against Muggles, certainly falls under wizarding jurisdiction. And indeed, Albus Dumbledore perfectly summarized this very rule when stating that: "All new wizards must accept that, in entering our world, they abide by our laws".[56]

The fact that crimes committed by witches and wizards always fall under wizarding jurisdiction also makes perfect sense. As stated earlier, try to image a police officer to restrain a witch to her cell even though she could simply use the *Alohomora* spell and walk out of there.

---

[52]Shaw (2017), pp. 497–499.

[53]More on this topic of jurisdiction in: Shaw (2017), pp. 488 ff.

[54]Rowling (1999), Chapter 2: Aunt Marge's Big Mistake.

[55]Rowling (1999), Chapter 3: The Knight Bus.

[56]Rowling (2005a), Chapter 13: The Secret Riddle.

2.4 How Do You Enforce International Law in Wizarding States?

It is one thing to understand if there is a violation of an international legal obligation. The next step is to know what can be done about this specific situation. In other words: if we know that the death eaters were violating fundamental rights of Muggles, Muggle-borns and others alike, what could be done about that? And what can be done if wizarding states violate their obligations? What if the Minister of Magic would be the perpetrator?

All these questions have become relevant in the context as well, over and over again. There are therefore different institutions that are in charge of dealing with violations of international law. Let's have a quick look at them to understand their role and limitations. Afterwards, we will do the same for the wizarding world.

2.4.1 Enforcement of International Law

There are a range of different entities in charge or resolving conflicts. They include political institutions such as the UN but also courts such as the ICJ, the International Criminal Court (ICC), regional courts but also international criminal tribunals such as the International Criminal Tribunal for the Former Yugoslavia (ICTY) or the International Criminal Tribunal for Rwanda (ICTR).[57] We won't go into details on all of the existing courts, tribunals, institutions. Instead, the goal is to provide you with a quick map on where to look for further information depending on the type of legal conflict you are looking into, with a focus on the courts and not the political institutions. So while the UN has an important role to play in resolving conflicts, they are focused on the political dimension and not on legal debates. We will therefore not look deeper into the role of the UN.

Instead, we will start with the ICJ, which can also be described as the "principal judicial organ of the United Nations".[58] The ICJ can decide upon legal disputes between two states or it can provide Advisory Opinions when it is requested to do so.[59] Private persons or international organizations cannot be brought before the ICJ.[60] Relevant cases for the ICJ would for example be if Britain and France were to have a border dispute. This would be a typical case for the ICJ.

In addition, there is a way to hold those people who have committed horrific acts such as crimes against humanity accountable. This can either happen before national courts or—if these national courts are "unwilling or unable"[61] in front of

---

[57] More on this in Chap. 5.

[58] Shaw (2017), p. 808. In this, he is referring to Art. 92 of the UN Charter. On the link between the ICJ and the political discussions on the same matter in front of the UN: Shaw (2017), p. 809.

[59] Shaw (2017), p. 813.

[60] Shaw (2017), pp. 813 ff.

[61] More on this criterion for the ICC to take over: Art. 17 Rome Statute.

international courts. There are different types of international courts in charge of these types of crimes. For some cases, the international community set up a court that was tackling only crimes in relation to one specific conflict. Examples are the International Criminal Tribunal for the former Yugoslavia (ICTY) as well as the International Criminal Tribunal for Rwanda (ICTR). These two war crimes tribunals were established by the UN Security Council. They were in charge of prosecuting individuals (not states) for the crimes they committed during the conflicts in former Yugoslavia as well as Rwanda.[62]

Such special tribunals for conflicts remain the exception. One alternative option to still reach justice is the ICC. The ICC can prosecute individuals for committing genocide, war crimes, crimes against humanity and the crime of aggression.[63] In order for the ICC to be able to prosecute individuals, certain conditions need to be met. To oversimplify—in order for the ICC to be able to prosecute, the state on which territory the acts occurred, or the state of which the person who is accused holds nationality, needs to be party to the ICC (meaning it needs to have signed and ratified the Rome Statute). The state needs to have been a party to the ICC during the time when the act occurred (so if the state joined a few months later, the individual cannot be tried in front of the ICC).[64] One exception is, if the UN Security Council refers a situation to the court.[65] We will discuss the different crimes that are mentioned here later when looking into specific examples from the wizarding world.

As mentioned earlier, there is also the option of prosecuting individuals before national courts. It is not possible to prosecute a state in front of a national court (as states are considered sovereign, this would lead to a whole bunch of other issues) but at least the heads of state or other high ranking officials can be held accountable, so long as their acts do not fall under the protection of immunity (this protection does not hold in worst crimes such as genocide, war crimes and crimes against humanity but it effectively hinders prosecution in other cases).[66]

2.4.2 Wizarding Enforcement Bodies

In the wizarding world, there is no mentioning of anything similar to the ICC or ICJ. While there are international organization such as the International Confederation of Wizards (of which Dumbledore was Supreme Mugwump), the judicial system seems to be limited to national institutions such as the Wizengamot in Britain. So for all those entrepreneurial witches and wizards out there—this is your chance to shine and

---

[62] More on both in: Shaw (2017), pp. 202 ff.

[63] This is laid down in Art. 5 of the Rome Statute. More details on the ICC come in a later chapter—if you cannot wait please jump to Sect. 5.1.

[64] More in: Shaw (2017), p. 298.

[65] Shaw (2017), p. 299.

[66] More on the concept of state immunity: van Alebeek (2008).

to develop a much needed system to bring those accountable of the most heinous crimes to justice across the globe.

2.5   Is There Such a Thing as Immunity in the Wizarding World?

2.5.1   What Does Immunity Mean?

Ever since global pandemics have become more than a Hollywood feature in doomsday movies, immunity as a term immediately leads to associations with diseases—yet, in this context, it has a completely different meaning. We talk about immunity from jurisdiction. Yes, you remember correctly. Jurisdiction is what we just looked into. Immunity is a bit like a shield charm against jurisdiction. It means that even though you (whether you are a state or a representative with diplomatic privileges) might have done something wrong, no one can pull you in front of a court and bring you to justice. This seems unfair! That is at least what I first exclaimed when I read about this in my early days of studying law. But let's go a bit deeper into this to understand where it comes from and what this means for the wizarding world. The reason for immunity is quite simple and relates to one of the initial principles we assessed: sovereignty of states. This is why—simply put—you can't pull a state in front of another state's court. Kind of makes sense. If you say that states are sovereign and are free to do as they please, pulling them in front of another state's court would counteract this sense of freedom. But what if one state is harming another state severely? Yes, there are of course exceptions and some ways in which states can be held accountable. This is where the ICJ and ICC come in, as we had discussed earlier—this is because the states consent to the authority of these judicial organs by ratifying their treaties.[67]

Another area of immunity that is very important is immunity of the state's representatives, such as high-ranking state officials (think Fudge) and diplomats (to different degrees). You will immediately think about parking tickets. At least for me—someone with very limited abilities in terms of parking—this always seemed like the prime perk to have as a diplomat. But this type of immunity was not intended to protect untalented people like me from prosecution if we don't park our car properly, while on a diplomatic posting in a foreign country (promise, I would never actually do that!)—it has deeper roots. The idea behind it is that during their terms/while holding their position high-raking state officials (meaning the president, prime minister etc.—again, think Fudge) and diplomats who are sent by one state to another nation are protected from being pulled in front of another state's court. This covers both official and private acts, as it needs to be ensured that no other state can make up a charge under which it can prosecute a president or diplomat of another state and throw them into jail. Just think an evil state run by the Squib twin sister of Umbridge who migrated to another country (luckily there are no reports of such a

---

[67]If you want to learn more about state immunity, check out this book: Fox and Webb (2013).

person, but you never know what they hushed up) and this twin sister is fighting with the prime minister of your country. If there were no diplomatic immunities, Umbridge's twin sister could just decide to take matters into her own hand and throw the ambassador of your country into jail to have political bargaining chip and get your country to do as she wants. This of course would be difficult for diplomatic relations among countries. So in order to avoid this from happening, states—in general of course—mutually respect the principle of diplomatic immunity.[68]

And then there is yet another type of immunity. As you may have noticed: if lawyers do something, they do it right—and complicated—in many cases. The third type of immunity is immunity linked to the acts of people. It is linked directly to the official acts of all state officials. The most important distinction here is between commercial and governmental action, in lawyer-lingo called *acta jure imperii* (yes, it has the ring of "empire" to it and means governmental action) and *acta jure gestionis* (no solid way of explaining this to you so just go with "it has to be the other one", which is commercial action). If you are working for a government, let's say are an employee in the Ministry of Finance on an official mission in another state, then you have immunity. So the other state can't put you in jail for any of the work you do on this official trip and in this official function linked to your government. If you decide to—in your free time—run over the cat of Umbridge's twin because you had a falling out during a meeting with her, this won't be understood as linked to your governmental action, but is your private problem. And it might lead to you having to pay a fine or worse.[69]

Now let's look at this again from a higher level. What we talked about are three different types of immunity: state immunity (also sometimes called sovereign immunity), immunity of state officials (fancy-lawyer term for this is immunity *ratione personae*—yes, you guessed correctly, this means "personal" immunity) and subject-matter immunity (immunity *ratione materiae*—don't ask me why we have to say this in Latin even though there is a decent English term for it). Let's try to understand whether any of these are relevant to the wizarding world.

2.5.2 Does Immunity Exist for Wizards?

It's a good question and one that we frankly don't have an answer to. There is no situation—at least to the author's knowledge, that eludes to anything such as immunity in the wizarding world. It would, however, make sense to assume that there is. At least among wizarding states, we should assume that they know the context of state immunity given that there are no accounts of states being able to force others in front of a domestic court. Regarding immunity of state officials, the only guess we can have is that it also exists. At least some type of protection. Think of the abuse of office that Fudge should be held liable for but isn't. While he was

---

[68] If you want to learn more about this type of immunity, check out: Webb (2012), p. 119.

[69] More on this in: Markus (2014), para 119–137.

officially relieved of his duty, he still continued to support the Ministry of Magic in an attempt to—let's assume the best—help clean up the mess that he created. But no one tried to officially charge him with misuse of office or anything worse. For subject-matter immunity, there is absolutely no evidence, so no clarity if this concept is known to the wizarding world or not.

References

Cambridge Dictionary (2022). https://dictionary.cambridge.org/us/dictionary/english/attribution. Accessed 5 Dec 2022

Cassese A (2007) The Nicaragua and Tadic tests revisited in light of the ICJ judgment on genocide in Bosnia. Eur J Int Law 18:649–668

CIA World Factbook (2022) Tuvalu. https://www.cia.gov/the-world-factbook/countries/tuvalu/#people-and-society. Accessed 5 Dec 2022

Condorelli L, Kress C (2010) The rules of attribution: general considerations. In: Crawford J et al (eds) The law of international responsibility. Oxford University Press, Oxford

Crawford J et al (2010) The law of international responsibility. Oxford University Press, Oxford

Fox H, Webb P (2013) The law of state immunity, 3rd edn. Oxford University Press, Oxford

Grimmelmann J (2012) Sealand, HavenCo and the rule of law. Univ Illinois Law Rev 2:405–484

ILC (2001) Draft articles on responsibility of states for internationally wrongful acts, with commentaries. UN Doc. A/56/10

Kolb R (2017) The international law of state responsibility: an introduction. Edward Elgar, Cheltenham

Mačák K (2016) Decoding Article 8 of the International Law Commission's articles on state responsibility: attribution of cyber operations by non-state actors. J Conflict Secur Law 21:405–428

Markus AR (2014) International Zivilprozessrecht. Stämpfli Verlag, Bern

Momtaz D (2010) Attribution of conduct to the state: state organs and entities empowered to exercise elements of governmental authority. In: Crawford J et al (eds) The law of international responsibility. Oxford University Press, Oxford

Renz F (2020) State responsibility and new trends in the privatization of warfare. Edward Elgar, Northampton

Rowling JK (1999) Harry Potter and the prisoner of Azkaban. Bloomsbury, London

Rowling JK (2005a) Harry Potter and the half-blood prince. Bloomsbury, London

Rowling JK (2005b) MuggleNet and Leaky Cauldron interview. https://www.mugglenet.com/2005/07/emerson-spartz-and-melissa-anelli-the-mugglenet-and-leaky-cauldron-interview-joanne-kathleen-rowling/. Accessed 5 Dec 2022

Rowling JK (2007) Harry Potter and the deathly hallows. Bloomsbury, London

Rowling JK (2015) Azkaban. https://www.wizardingworld.com/writing-by-jk-rowling/azkaban. Accessed 10 Dec 2022

Rowling JK (2016) Seventeenth century and beyond. https://www.wizardingworld.com/writing-by-jk-rowling/seventeenth-century-and-beyond-en. Accessed 1 Feb 2022

Rowling JK, Whisp K (n.d.) Quidditch through the ages

Shaw MN (2017) International law, 8th edn. Cambridge University Press, Cambridge

van Alebeek R (2008) The immunity of states and their officials in international criminal law and international human rights law. Oxford University Press, Oxford

Webb P (2012) Human rights and the immunities of state officials. In: De Wet E, Vidmar J (eds) Hierarchy in international law: the place of human rights. Oxford University Press, Oxford, pp 114–147

Wellingtongoose (2015) Wizards – an endangered species. http://wellingtongoose.tumblr.com/post/109915776984/wizards-an-endangered-species. Accessed 5 Dec 2022

International Humanitarian Law

3

Abstract

The wizarding world is full of conflict—at least during bad years, meaning pretty much whenever Grindelwald or Voldemort are on the loose. During those years, wizards have to confront questions everyone else has to answer when watching the news: are those groups terrorists or freedom fighters, what kind of conflict are we facing, what are the rights of those fighting in this conflict or affected by it? Let us jointly take a look at how those questions are answered in our world. After that, we will of course try to understand how this can be applied to the wizarding world.

3.1 What Is International Humanitarian Law?

International Humanitarian Law (IHL) is the law governing armed conflicts, also called "Law of Armed Conflict". Some of you might be sitting in front of this book thinking "this is stupid, no one is following rules during war". You're not alone with this sentiment. Indeed, it was Cicero who reportedly stated "*inter arma leges silent*", meaning during times of war, the laws are silent (and yay to Latin classes).[1] And while opposing Cicero might feel like overstepping my boundaries of wisdom (well frankly, no, it feels quite all right), this is an oversimplification. There are laws in war and the laws are far from silent. This does not mean that the laws I'll present you on the following pages are always followed. No law is. Otherwise, plenty of lawyers would be unemployed. Of course, there are various groups that violate IHL. There are also several states that show a blatant disregard for the laws of war. The same is also true if you look at the smaller scale in your own cities. There are people who steal, bribe, cheat on contracts, harm others. Yet, hardly anyone would argue that having a legal system in place which serves as our guardrail for what is right and

---

[1] Solis (2010), p. 3.

what is wrong would be a waste of time. If someone breaks the law, they have to face the consequences. Let us later check whether this also holds true regarding the laws of war.[2]

3.1.1   Sources of International Humanitarian Law

The development of IHL started in the middle of the nineteenth century. Among the first sources of IHL was the Geneva Convention for the Amelioration of the Condition of the Wounded in Armies in the Field. The Convention was signed at the initiative of Henry Dunant, who had seen the horrors of the battle of Solferino.[3] Based on his initiative, the International Committee of the Red Cross (ICRC) was founded.[4] Think of the ICRC as a neutral, unarmed Order of the Phoenix dedicated to the protection of victims during armed conflicts.

There were many further developments which won't be listed fully here. The key conventions any decent lawyer has to remember are the Hague Conventions as well as the Geneva Conventions. The Hague Conventions describe treaties and declarations that contain rules regulating warfare, mainly focused on the use of means and methods of warfare, the conduct of hostilities and occupation. The Geneva Conventions focus on the protection of victims and nowadays refer to the four Geneva Conventions as well as the Additional Protocols.[5] These legal treaties (meaning documents signed by several if not all nations) are the foundation of IHL. For simplicity sake, we'll leave it at that for the moment. Should you decide to further study this fascinating issue and become a true lawyer, please remember that any introductory work is not aimed at providing you a full picture but a first glimpse at a topic. So don't be surprised if you happen to stumble upon customary international law that also regulates armed conflicts and find a variety of additional treaties to consider.[6]

---

[2] Side note for the cynics among you: even if we only focus on the "symbolic" effect of the law, it turns out that adherence to IHL is an argument for some rebel groups when requesting support from the international community. More on this fascinating issue in Jo (2015). So let's focus on this bright side when diving into the debate of what IHL is about and what it means when applied to the wizarding world.

[3] Venturing into the general realm of book recommendations now but I can highly recommend to read more about the life and work of Henry Dunant in the book: Hasler (1994).

[4] More on this in: Shaw (2017), p. 892.

[5] For more details on the sources of IHL refer to ibid., pp. 892 ff. For an overview into the development of IHL, look into Solis (2010), p. 3 ff.

[6] A brief overview of custom as a source of IHL is given by Solis (2010), pp. 12 ff.

3.1.2   International Humanitarian Law as Lex Specialis

IHL is often times considered as *lex specialis*. This concept is actually quite fascinating to understand. First, it is important to understand that IHL does not always apply. Now why is that? IHL specifically addresses rules for situations of armed conflict. Should they differ from peace time rules? Let's think of an easy example. Let's say a coworker of Vernon Dursley in his drill-making company is running amok in Surrey. If the police were to encounter this coworker, they would try to capture, not kill him. Actually, aiming to kill him would only be ok in case of an absolute necessity. Under IHL, there is no requirement to aim for capture as killing is seen as an inevitable aspect of waging war, if—and that is the big question—the person targeted is a combatant or a civilian directly participating in hostilities. Yes, I know this is vastly oversimplified. But you'll get the idea—there are some things you can do in a conflict you would not be allowed to do in a non-conflict setting. That's what this is all about.

Before we go into any of the details, we need to understand when IHL is the relevant legal framework and when the focus is on international human rights law. In general, as soon as there is an armed conflict, IHL applies as the law is especially designed for these circumstances (hence *lex specialis*). Of course, life is not as easy and black and white as that. So there are many exceptions.[7] But our focus will be on this main criterion. The rest is a matter for a closer look once it becomes relevant.

3.2   What Types of Conflicts Exist in the Wizarding World?

3.2.1   International and Non-International Armed Conflicts in IHL

There are two types of conflicts: international armed conflicts (IAC) and non-international armed conflicts (NIAC). After the Peace Treaty of Westphalia in 1648 there was agreement that the new go-to-solution would be sovereign nation states. As IHL was written in the post-Westphalian era, most of its norms therefore address IAC, meaning conflicts between two states.[8] While it might seem like a distinction designed to keep lawyers busy, it has real-life consequences for many people affected by armed conflicts. So, let's have a look at what these two types of conflict are.

3.2.1.1   International Armed Conflict
IAC means that two states fight one another. This requires the use of armed force by a state through its military or private actors against another state in that state's

---

[7] The relationship between IHL and international human rights law is brilliantly laid out in: Sassòli and Olson (2008).

[8] Akande (2012), p. 40; Melzer (2008), pp. 244 ff.

territory.[9] Wow that was a lot to take in. In simpler terms: one state needs to use force against another state. This can be done via the military (old school) or other actors such as a private military company (new trend in warfare, think scourers going rogue based on orders from another nation).[10] The conflict does not need to have a predefined length (i.e. 2 weeks) and it does not need to cover a specific territory (i.e. 2 ha). No one needs to formally declare war. So far so good.

Yet, lawyers like to establish different theories to complicate legal matters even further. With regards to the classification of armed conflicts, one of the theoretical debates is about when the armed conflict started. A famous lawyer, Jean S. Pictet, stated that no formal declaration of war is necessary, but that every hostile act or a single wounded person is sufficient to trigger the application of the Geneva Conventions (GC).[11] This "first shot theory" (given the lack of wands to use) is convincing. Every other measure would allow states to escalate situations without IHL being applicable.[12] I'll therefore spare you a deep dive into all other theories there are. This is not only ok as I am writing this book and you'll therefore have to trust my judgment, but also because this view was upheld by the ICTY in the 1995 *Tadić Interlocutory Appeal.*[13] Lawyers like to rely on judgments by international courts to affirm the opinion held by legal scholars. It is quite a dance. Scholars develop theories, these theories are followed by the courts and cited in other books and journal articles. If many other scholars and courts follow your opinion, it is considered a leading opinion. This means you win the argument. Until another scholar develops a better theory. Then it starts again.[14]

---

[9]Geneva Convention for the Amelioration of the Condition of the Wounded and Sick in Armed Forces in the Field of 12 August 1949, UNTS Vol. 75, I-970; Geneva Convention for the Amelioration of the Condition of Wounded, Sick and Shipwrecked Members of Armed Forces at Sea of 12 August 1949, UNTS Vol. 75, I-971; Geneva Convention Relative to the Treatment of Prisoners of War of 12 August 1949, UNTS Vol. 75, I-972; Geneva Convention Relative to the Protection of Civilian Persons in Time of War of 12 August 1949, UNTS Vol. 75, I-973, common art 2. ICRC, *Commentary on the First Geneva Convention: Convention (I) for the Amelioration of the Condition of the Wounded and Sick in Armed Forces in the Field* (updated commentary, ICRC 2016) paras 202, 210–211. More on this in Solis (2010), p. 150.

[10]If the idea of scourers only confuses you further, please look them up here: Rowling (2016), Seventeenth Century and Beyond.

[11]Pictet (1952), p. 32.

[12]On the goal of IHL to mitigate suffering: Cassese (2014), p. 5.

[13]ICTY, *Prosecutor v. Dusko Tadić a/k/a 'Dule'*, IT-94-1, Appeals Chamber, Decision on the Defense Motion for Interlocutory Appeal on Jurisdiction, 2 October 1995 § 70.

[14]Some scholars are particularly clever and have developed a special trick: by quoting themselves and their books in new publications, they drive up the understanding that theirs is the leading opinion. Quite smart. Instead of just saying "I thought about this issue in the same way while standing in the kitchen, the bathroom and the living room" you just repeat the same argument in different academic publications and the number of times it is written brings it closer to being considered the correct opinion.

3.2.1.2 Non-international Armed Conflict

In the last decades, states have seen more and more NIAC.[15] Determining the threshold of when it is a NIAC is more difficult. In those conflicts, several scenarios are possible. These scenarios involve not only armed groups and foreign governments intervening alongside civilian populations, but also private contractors.[16] Fortunately, IHL recognizes the possibility of categorizing conflicts as internationalized or mixed conflicts with both international and non-international components.[17] Internal disturbances and tensions, including riots or isolated and sporadic acts of violence are below the threshold of a NIAC based on the definition in Common Art. 3 GC I-IV (it is called Common Art. 3 because the same article is included in all four GCs).[18] There are two key requirements for NIAC under Common Art. 3 GC I-IV.

1. The hostilities have to reach a **minimum level of intensity**. This means, yes, you guessed it, mere use of swear words is not enough. An indicator of this minimum level of intensity is if the state has to use military force to respond to the acts of violence instead of just using police forces.
2. The non-governmental groups have to be **"parties to the conflict"**, which means they have to be organized armed forces. Organized armed forces means that it is not sufficient if two individuals decide to wreak havoc, it has to be a group with a certain command structure that would be able to sustain military operations.[19]

3.2.1.3 Why Conflict Classification Matters

But why does the type of conflict matter? Well, as the rules of war were written for IAC, significantly more legal rules apply to these types of conflicts. In a NIAC, only Common Art. 3 GC I-IV and Additional Protocol (AP) II apply.[20] There are differences in particular related to detention and prosecution.[21] But then, as always in international law, that is not the end of the story. Other rules, which were written for IAC, are applicable as customary international law; remember, this was the term I mentioned before and used it to nudge you to fully study international law—we'll keep it like that. If you want to learn more and are looking for some "light reading" as Hermione would say, I can only recommend the relevant works by the ICRC on this issue.[22]

---

[15] For a detailed study of conflict trends: Allansson et al. (2017), pp. 574 ff.

[16] Bernard (2014), p. 5.

[17] Turns (2014), pp. 821, 827.

[18] On the threshold of a NIAC based on Art. 1 Additional Protocol (AP) II: Solis (2010), pp. 163 ff.; Sandoz et al. (1987), N 4464 ff.

[19] More on this in: Solis (2010), pp. 204 ff.

[20] ibid., p. 149.

[21] Shaw (2017), p. 914.

[22] Henckaerts and Doswald-Beck (2005).

3.2.2   Conflict Classification in the Wizarding World

Now on to the really important question: what kind of conflict are we facing in the wizarding world? Within the wizarding world, there have been no remarks about conflicts between different wizarding nations. There do, however, seem to be quite frequent brawls between different magical creatures and wizards or within wizarding factions. The most well-known conflict is the Second Wizarding War. We'll take this conflict as the example to assess dynamics in the wizarding world.

When trying to understand the type of conflict between death eaters and the "rest" of the wizarding world, one needs to revert to the basic distinction between IAC and NIAC under IHL. We have to take a look at IHL because there is no known law of armed conflict in the wizarding world.

It is particularly important not to fall into the same trap as many politicians tend to: declaring war whenever they feel like it (from a war against drugs to a war against terrorism and finally the war against Christmas, there are varying degrees of inaccuracy and lack of any basic legal understanding associated with the terminology).

When looking at the previous classification of armed conflicts, we have to differentiate between IAC and NIAC. The first distinction is easiest: it is clearly not an IAC, as there are not two wizarding states facing off against one another. It is also not a situation in which one wizarding nation is fighting a Muggle nation. This would also classify as an IAC. While fascinating, for everyone's sake, I hope that this scenario will be avoided in the future. Conflicts among Muggles or among wizards are nasty enough, adding more complexity (and magic) to those situations is really not necessary.

When asking the question of whether the conflict between the death eaters and the "rest" of the wizarding world classifies as a NIAC, we'll have to distinguish four phases of the conflict. We'll ignore the acts of the death eaters against the Muggles as the list below will already give you a sense of the whole range of conflict classifications.

3.2.2.1 Activities of the Death Eaters Prior to the Return of Voldemort

The first phase we will have to classify is the phase prior to the return of Voldemort. From the moment of Voldemort's disappearance, there was a long period in which the death eaters were in hiding or continued their normal lives, believing their leader to be dead. This was true for many of his loyal followers such as Lucius Malfoy.[23]

The end of this relative calm was the reappearance of the Dark Mark during the Quidditch World Cup. During this event, a group of death eaters stormed the campsite and destroyed everything they encountered. They tortured Muggles and Muggle-borns witches and wizards alike. At the end of the riot, Barty Crouch

---

[23] Others, such as Bellatrix Lestrange, continued to believe he was alive. Whether this was out of true loyalty, intuition or the desperate desire to hold on to the belief while being surrounded by dementors in Azkaban will be left for others to answer.

Jr. fired the Dark Mark into the sky and disapparated. This riot was the first instance in which the death eaters were visibly active and displaying their loyalty to Voldemort after his initial disappearance years earlier. Do these acts already suffice to classify it as an armed conflict?

As mentioned before, sporadic acts of violence are not considered an armed conflict. While appalling in their nature, the acts of the death eaters during the Quidditch World Cup as well as the isolated acts before Voldemort's return do not reach the minimum level of intensity and the death eaters are not an organized armed group before Voldemort returns. The activities of the death eaters prior to Voldemort's return can therefore not be considered a NIAC.

3.2.2.2 The First Year After Voldemort's Return

The second phase we will look at is the first year after Voldemort's return. This year was marked by the wizarding community's unwillingness to accept his return as a fact. The Ministry of Magic and Minister of Magic Fudge in particular focused their energy on denouncing the claims of Professor Dumbledore and Harry that Voldemort had returned.[24] Meanwhile, Voldemort was lying low and building up his base of followers.

During this phase, there was no open conflict involving Voldemort and his death eaters. There was therefore also no NIAC based on the understanding of law of armed conflict.

3.2.2.3 From the Battle in the Ministry of Magic to the Fall of the Ministry

The third phase extends from the Battle in the Ministry of Magic to the fall of the Ministry. The nature of the conflict changed with the battle in the Ministry of Magic and the first open acts of violence by death eaters against not only members of the Order of the Phoenix but also the Aurors which were summoned by Professor Dumbledore.

The Battle in the Ministry of Magic was a gamechanger not only regarding the Ministry of Magic's realization that something was seriously wrong with their assumption about Voldemort's non-existence. It was also a gamechanger regarding the classification of the conflict between the death eaters and the Ministry of Magic.

After the Battle in the Ministry of Magic during which Sirius Black was killed, the death eaters moved out into the open and wreaked havoc. They were involved in the Brockdale bridge destruction, two very nasty murders, the supposed hurricane in the West Country (the Obliviators were doing their best work on memory charms so

---

[24] In an effort to stop Professor Dumbledore from spreading the news about Voldemort's return, the Ministry of Magic had him voted out of the Chairmanship of the International Confederation of Wizards (arguing he were too old and losing his grip), demoted him from Chief Warlock on the Wizengamot (the Wizard's High Court) and were considering taking away his Order of Merlin, First Class. More on this in: Rowling (2003), Chapter 8: The Hearing.

the Muggles forgot about the giants' involvement in the destruction) and the madness of Junior Minister Herbert Chorley.[25]

The next year saw an increase in violence throughout the country. This violence paralleled the developments of Voldemort's first rise to power. During this year, the Ministry of Magic was under the leadership of Minister Rufus Scrimgeour. He was clearly aware of the rise of Voldemort and understood it as a core threat. As mentioned previously, Scrimgeour even pointed out to the Muggle Prime Minister that they were at war against the death eaters and Voldemort. But how should this conflict be classified—legally, not for PR purposes? And is a war against non-state actors even possible?

Let us first take a look at the parties involved at this stage. On the one hand is the Ministry of Magic in the slightly more competent hands of Rufus Scrimgeour.[26] On the other hand are the death eaters following Voldemort.

As was previously discussed, the wizarding world in Britain is considered a state of its own right. The only remaining question is therefore how to classify the death eaters. They are certainly not a state. This makes them by default a non-state actor.

Based on a judgment by the ICTY (here we go again), the key factors to determine whether a conflict falls under the definition of a NIAC are the intensity of the conflict and the organization of the parties to the conflict.[27]

Lawyers define the minimum level of organization as: "the existence of a command structure and disciplinary rules and mechanisms within the group; the existence of a headquarters; the fact that the group controls a certain territory; the ability of the group to gain access to weapons, other military equipment, recruits and military training; its ability to plan, coordinate and carry out military operations, including troop movements and logistics; its ability to define a unified military strategy and use military tactics; and its ability to speak with one voice and negotiate and conclude agreements such as cease-fire or peace accords."[28]

Let us apply this to the death eaters. The death eaters have a crystal-clear command structure (Voldemort commands, the rest acts), disciplinary rules and mechanisms are in place (you go against Voldemort's orders, you are punished and might die). They have a headquarter (wherever Voldemort resides), have access to wands (therefore weapons access) and speak with one voice (well, Voldemort does at least). The other criteria are not that easy to determine for this first phase (but let's keep this discussion in mind for the next phase of the conflict).

Before trying to understand what the sufficient level of organization of the death eaters is, let us have a brief look at the threshold of intensity. And yes, we're taking

---

[25] Rowling (2005), Chapter 1: The Other Minister.

[26] Well, if you compare to Fudge, many people appear competent. But so is life, we will all have numerous examples in our head of recent elections where we thought "Well, he/she may not be perfect, but certainly better than . . .". So let's not discuss this further but keep the issue of dwelling on the mediocracy of so many elected official for another day.

[27] ICTY, Prosecutor v Tadic, IT-94-1-T, Judgment (7 May 1997), para 562.

[28] ICTY, The Prosecutor v. Ramush Haradinaj et al., Trial Chamber I (Judgment), Case No. IT-04-84-T, 3 April 2008, para. 60. See also ICRC (2008), p. 3. More on this in: Melzer (2016), p. 69.

the lazy way out here—instead of finishing the discussion on the first critical element I'll now show you why it is not an IAC as there is no sufficient intensity of the conflict (yet). This might not be intellectually satisfying to some of you as you would have liked to finish the first discussion. But it is the easy way out and I'm a pragmatic person.

The conflict needs to have a certain level of intensity. Why is that? Well, there are simply sufficient situations in which national criminal law and human rights law is best able to cover the conflict e.g., between a government and a group of criminals. NIACs are more than riots, isolated and sporadic acts of violence or other similar events, as we had mentioned before.[29] Factors to be considered include among many others the "number, duration and intensity of individual confrontations; the type of weapons and other military equipment used; the number and calibre of munitions fired; the number of persons and type of forces partaking in the fighting; the number of casualties; the extent of material destruction; and the number of civilians fleeing combat zones".[30] Granted, munitions and types of weapons are not really applicable here. But for the rest it seems that the few incidents mentioned before don't live up to the intensity required here. This first phase in which the death eaters operate openly therefore is not considered as living up to the intensity requirement of a NIAC. As horrible as the sporadic acts of violence are, they do not live up to the required intensity justifying a shift away from national criminal law and human rights law to IHL.

In fact, it seemed that declaring war on the death eaters was more a publicity stunt to make up for the year in which the Ministry of Magic failed to respond to the return of Voldemort and the ascent of the death eaters. They continued to make random arrests (Stan Shunpike being the key example during that phase) and focused on cover ups of breakouts instead of fully addressing Voldemort's second rise to power.

3.2.3 The Fall of the Ministry of Magic Until the Battle of Hogwarts

The last phase we will have to assess is after the fall of the Ministry of Magic leading up to the Battle of Hogwarts. Prior to their coup, the death eaters were using the *Imperius* Curse to control civil servants high up in the ranks of the Ministry of Magic. This included Pius Thicknesse who was Head of the Department of Magical Law Enforcement. Ultimately, this lead to the death eaters assassinating Rufus Scrimgeour (after torturing him for information about Harry Potter's whereabouts, which he did not give up) and placing Pius Thicknesse in his place. During the brief battle, the death eaters defeated the Ministry officials as well as the Aurors and took control of the headquarters in London. From this moment on, the Ministry of Magic acted in line with the death eaters and carried out horrible acts on their behalf. For instance, the Ministry of Magic created the Muggle-Born Registration Commission

---

[29] ibid., p. 70.

[30] ICTY, The Prosecutor v. Ramush Haradinaj et al., para. 49.

which imprisoned innocent Muggle-borns in Azkaban. To make the coup perfect, Voldemort and his army of death eaters also took control over the Daily Prophet and used this to spread misinformation against Harry Potter and the members of the Order of the Phoenix.

So the question is: what does a coup mean and how does this coup impact the assessment of the underlying conflict? In the Muggle world, coups don't involve civil servants being placed under the *Imperius* Curse. However, to many of them, the situation might feel similar. At least in dictatorships, which remain most prone to coups, the level in which civil servants stand to gain when resisting the incoming "new dictator" is also highly limited.[31] The official version of the coup also remained that Scrimgeour had resigned. This way, it was expected that there would be less resistance against the takeover.

With this *de facto* regime change, the classification of the conflict also undergoes a certain change. Suddenly, it is no longer the death eaters and Voldemort fighting against the Ministry of Magic and groups such as the Order of the Phoenix. Now, the Order of the Phoenix is part of the resistance and the Ministry of Magic belongs to the Voldemort and the death eaters.[32]

As mentioned before, such a reversal in roles from opposition/rebel forces to new government and from previously in charge to resistance is not uncommon, especially in dictatorships. Our task will be to understand what this means for the classification of the conflict.

Right after the fall of the Ministry of Magic, the entire Order of the Phoenix—the key group resisting Voldemort and his regime of terror—is scattered.[33] While in hiding, the members of the Order of the Phoenix do not engage in coordinated active acts of violence but are an underground resistance, participating in the radio program Potterwatch and encouraging people to protect innocent Muggles and Muggle-borns. During these months, there is no IAC or NIAC, as the acts of the Order of the Phoenix do not fulfill the intensity requirement of the NIAC.

This changes with the Battle of Hogwarts. The members of Dumbledore's Army (let us discuss their status later[34]) alongside the Order of the Phoenix formulated a battle plan together with the professors of Hogwarts. They organized the defense of the several entry points (school entrance, passageways) and engaged in a severe

---

[31] More on the fascinating dynamics with regards to the survival of dictatorships and coups that replace them: de Mesquita and Smith (2011).

[32] If you think this switch is confusing and does not make sense, I recommend reading up on the NIAC going on in the Central African Republic (with many groups working together, then finding new alliances). Conflicts are messy, so is their classification. More on this on the RULAC website. If you find this topic fascinating, I recommend browsing through the RULAC website of the Geneva Academy of International Humanitarian Law and Human Rights. The RULAC online portal qualifies situations of armed conflict, identifies parties to the conflict and monitors over 80 armed conflicts.

[33] More on this in Rowling (2007), Chapter 9: A Place to Hide; Rowling (2007), Chapter 14: The Thief.

[34] If you cannot wait for it, check out Sect. 3.4.2.

battle against the death eaters that drew heavy casualties on both sides. The phase around the Battle of Hogwarts constitutes a NIAC as Voldemort and his followers are in control of the Ministry of Magic and are thereby considered the state in this scenario. Even though Pius Thicknesse, the Minister of Magic at the time of the Battle of Hogwarts, only acted under the *Imperius* curse, the majority of the Ministry was under the control of Voldemort and the sole reason why he himself was not acting as Minister of Magic was that there was no necessity given that Thicknesse was under his effective control and taking care of it.

To sum up (lawyers love to do that to make sure you catch the key argument as they know they just hit you with way too many details): with the Fall of the Ministry of Magic, the roles reverse. Voldemort and the Death eaters control the government, the Order of the Phoenix is part of the underground resistance. During the initial months, the underground resistance is not actively fighting the death eaters and Voldemort, there is thus (very lawyerly) no conflict. This changes with the Battle of Hogwarts, when a NIAC between Voldemort and the death eaters on the one side and the Order of the Phoenix (as the armed rebel group) along with sympathizers, Dumbledore's Army and the teachers of Hogwarts breaks out.

3.3 Legal Status During Armed Conflicts

Are the death eaters combatants or civilians directly participating in hostilities? And what about the Order of the Phoenix? Fascinating questions if you ask me—but why would you care about the legal status of this adapted version of the Ku-Klux-Klan? The legal status is not all unlike a status with a hotel chain or airline where you're happy when reaching the free breakfast status or can use the lounge for free that you then never have time to visit (this is the consultant in me speaking now). Status—be it with a hotel chain or under IHL—determines the rights you have in a given situation. While the status for a hotel chain only promises mundane (yet yummy) benefits such as Nutella pancakes, the legal status under IHL determines what rights the people have and what role they play during the conflict. This also means it determines who can rightfully be attacked during the conflict. So going back to our adapted Ku-Klux-Klan called the death eaters, it will be important to understand what the status of the death eaters is to understand whether they were violating IHL. Before anyone cries foul—we'll do the same assessment for the Order of the Phoenix as well. So any Voldemort fans among you (though we should really have a talk about your moral compass)—this is not your average biased fake news mainstream media speaking, we'll take a look at all sides (and if you also don't feel the sarcasm in this sentence let's have a talk about the fake news debates some time).

As we don't know whether there are any wizarding rules on status during armed conflicts, we'll have to revert back to IHL to understand what this debate is about. As this is only an introduction to the most relevant principles, we will not go into all the details about the status of individuals under IHL but will focus on the most relevant issues. This boils down to two core discussions: (1) what is the distinction between combatants and civilians and (2) when are civilians considered as directly participating in hostilities.

3.3.1   Combatants and Civilians

The core divide in IHL—which is relevant for IAC—is that between combatants and civilians. A core principle of IHL is the protection of civilians from unnecessary suffering.[35] It is therefore important to understand who is a civilian, and who is not. For this, let us first understand who is considered a combatant.

Under IHL, combatants are members of the armed forces. They have the right to directly participate in hostilities (combatants' privilege). This might sound trivial but what does this really mean? It means that if country A and country B are in an IAC and a soldier of country A kills a soldier of country B, the soldier of country A does not have to fear to be tried for murder because of this act. Instead, his act falls under IHL. So long as the act is conform to the rules of IHL, the soldier does not have to fear criminal prosecution. Additionally, the combatants have the right to prisoner of war (POW) status once captured, offering them additional protection. We will not go further into the POW debate here as, frankly, there are no reports of wizards taking POWs.[36]

The downside of being considered a combatant is that one is a legitimate target even when not fighting. Imagine a group of soldiers at sleep and dreaming of their acceptance letters to Hogwarts—they might not seem like a danger to anyone in this moment but would still be legitimate targets given their status as combatants. The only exception is once a combatant is out of the fight for example because of an injury. In these cases, the combatants are considered *hors de combat* (yes, we're also mixing in French now—this means you are out of the battle, most likely as you are injured).

There are some additional groups which can be considered combatants alongside members of the military. These are e.g. members of militias or organized resistance movements which belong to a party of the conflict (all of this only being relevant to IAC) if they fulfill certain requirements regarding their command structure, fixed distinctive signs (meaning usually military uniforms), carrying their arms openly and acting in accordance with IHL.[37] As you might have been able to guess, not all of that will be applicable to the wizarding world. Some of these aspects might be completely unproblematic. All wizards usually run around with their wand out in the open. So much for carrying your arms openly. On other aspects, we'll need to think a bit longer before coming to any conclusions.

Aside from these groups, everyone who is not a combatant is per default considered a civilian during an armed conflict. As we know, that the wizarding

---

[35] Solis (2010), p. 269.

[36] If you want to learn more about POW status, please read up on it here: ibid. pp. 187 ff.

[37] More on all of this in Art. 4A II GC III as well as Art. 43 and 44 API I.

world is not facing an IAC, but a NIAC. Therefore, we will not have to assess whether there are any combatants in the wizarding world. But the question whether we see civilians directly participant in hostilities will be essential. So let's dive into that.

3.3.2 Civilians Directly Participating in Hostilities

As we mentioned before, because we are only looking at NIAC, the most relevant question will be whether the civilians are directly participating in hostilities. If you have never heard of this before, don't worry. Direct participation in hostilities is a relevant concept as even if you are a civilian during an armed conflict, you are not allowed to do whatever you want without fear of repercussions. As highlighted earlier, civilians are generally protected from direct attack. Yet, we are talking about law and as you might have already gathered, there is an exception to everything. This is also the case here. The relevant exception in this case is that civilians only enjoy protection from direct attack under Art. 51 III AP I and Art. 13 III AP II "unless and for such time as they take a direct part in hostilities".[38] The idea is quite simple—you misbehave, you can be punished. But in an armed conflict, no one is sent to the Forbidden Forest with Hagrid and Fang. Instead, if you attack others even while you are a civilian, you become a legitimate target.

Lawyers will tell you that this concept of direct participation in hostilities is vital in upholding the principle of distinction (meaning we distinguish those who fight from those we protect).[39] This means, that we only know who can be lawfully targeted during an armed conflict if we understand when a civilian is directly participating in hostilities.[40] As a side note—civilians directly participating in hostilities make the life of everyone more complicated, whether combatants, other fighters, or lawyers analyzing their status.[41] Yet, taking part in hostilities is neither considered a war crime nor generally forbidden.[42]

---

[38] This notion is also considered customary international law and corresponds to the provision of common Art. 3 GC I-IV stating that protection is granted to persons taking 'no active part in the hostilities'. See also Henckaerts and Doswald-Beck (2005), p. 20.

[39] You can find a more sophisticated explanation of the principle of distinction here: Solis (2010), p. 251.

[40] Akande (2010), p. 181; Watkin (2005), pp. 137, 139–140.

[41] For a general overview on the problems of the principle of distinction and civilians directly participating in hostilities: von Devivere (2008), pp. 24–47; Schmitt (2005), p. 539.

[42] The opposite view was held in early case law, particularly in: Nuremberg Military Tribunal, *United States v. List*, Nuremberg, 8 July 1948 to 19 February 1949, Law Reports of Trials of War Criminals Vol. VIII, United Nations Wartime Commission, London 1949 58. The common understanding is by now that there should not be a literal reading of the judgment but that it should be interpreted as stating that such unprivileged acts might lead to prosecution on a domestic level. Some do however still hold a differing view, stating that direct participation in hostilities amounts to a war crime and thus might be punishable even if there is no IHL violation. This view is among

A civilian (imagine one of Uncle Vernon's coworkers who by some misfortune ended up in the zone of a NIAC while promoting drills to the local government) is directly participating in hostilities if three elements are given:

– the threshold of harm,
– the direct causation between the act and the harm inflicted,
– the belligerent nexus.[43]

Let's take a look at all those elements one by one.

The **threshold of harm** means it has to hurt the other side. Or, in legal speak, it has to adversely affect the military operations or capacity of a conflict party or inflict death or injury to persons or destroy objects which are protected against such a direct attack.[44] If the action leads to death, injury or destruction it does not matter if this negatively affects the military operations (meaning you don't have to hit the most important commander, anyone related to the conflict will do). And it is also enough if there is an "objective likelihood" of the harm being inflicted. Meaning even if you might miss, it can still qualify.[45]

Direct causation between the act and the harm inflicted means—you guessed it—there needs to be a direct causal link. Let's look at this in comparison to acts sustaining the war effort. If you produce weapons, construct roads that lead tanks to the battlefield or provide logistical services you are helping sustain the war effort.[46] But would you feel like directly participating in hostilities? Likely not. For this, you need to be closer to the action. Not in terms of location but in terms of your actions and their link to hostilities. There needs to be only "one causal step" between the act and the harm that is inflicted.[47] The reason for this is that if you would count all acts sustaining the war effort as direct participation in hostilities, a wide range of people would lose their protection and you would fully erode the principle of distinction.[48] The causal link should, however, also not be overstated. It does not have to be an indispensable contribution (so you don't have to pull the trigger or drop the bomb).[49] But you have to do more than just transporting weapons.

The **belligerent nexus** exists to ensure that the act is designed to harm one party of the armed conflict while supporting the other party. At the essence it means that if you kill your neighbor during an armed conflict because your fence issue is still not

others reflect in the US Manual for Military Commissions and further elaborated on in: Crawford (2015), p. 132.
[43] These are not elements that I came up with myself. They are part of the ICRC Guidance on Direct Participation in Hostilities. Please verify in: Melzer (2009), p. 46; Lesh (2016), pp. 181–186.
[44] Melzer (2009), p. 47.
[45] Solis (2010), p. 218. See further: Schmitt (2010), p. 725.
[46] On the importance of this distinction: Sandoz et al. (1987), p. 619.
[47] Melzer (2009), p. 58.
[48] ibid., p. 52; Akande (2012), p. 188.
[49] Schmitt (2010), p. 728.

resolved, this will not have the required belligerent nexus but is just a shitty move that will earn you punishment under national criminal law. But at least you are not considered a civilian participating in hostilities and the other party to the conflict can't legally attack you (you can see, I'm always the optimist).[50]

If civilians fulfill all of these cumulative criteria, they lose their protection for the time of their participation in hostilities. After their direct participation ends, they are again granted protection as civilians (the "'revolving door' of civilian protection").[51] It is a "temporary, activity-based loss of protection".[52]

There is, you guessed it, an exception to this. If civilians regularly directly participate in hostilities and are considered members of an armed group (in legal speak if the "person assumes a continuous function for the group, involving his or her direct participation in hostilities"),[53] they no longer have the revolving door benefit.[54] The underlying rationale is that it would be unrealistic to expect a state's armed forces to wait until the members of the rebel group have picked up their weapons again before being allowed to attack.[55] The classic example to the contrary, allowing for the revolving door, would lead to the 'farmer by day, fighter by night' scenario.[56] This is avoided with the category for members of an armed group. Now, there will be few witches and wizards who are farmers by day and fighters by night but consider the scenario of "Selling Hogwarts robes by day, fighting the Ministry of Magic by night"—not much better. Members of an armed group lose their protection for as long as they have their role with a continuous combat function within this armed group. I won't go any deeper into the criteria for renouncing your combat role and taking up a desk job (yes, that option exists)—but if you do, you can regain your civilian protection as long as you don't fall back into old patterns.[57]

3.3.3 And What Does This Mean for the Death Eaters?

As you will all know, the death eaters are Voldemort's fan club and army of murderous Muggle haters.[58] Now let's aim to understand the status of the death

---

[50] ibid., pp. 735–736.

[51] Melzer (2009), p. 70.

[52] ibid.

[53] ibid., p. 33.

[54] On this loss of the revolving door benefit: Lewis and Crawford (2013), p. 1148.

[55] See Cameron and Chetail (2013), p. 413.

[56] On this example: Schmitt (2005), p. 535. If members of an armed group want to regain their protection as civilians, they have to disengage from their continuous combat function, whereby it suffices if they just take up a different role in the group such as administrative tasks: Melzer (2009), p. 72.

[57] More on this concept of having a continuous combat function: Solis (2010), p. 205.

[58] The death eaters conveniently have a group tattoo on their arm. So in case it is decently warm in Britain and all death eaters have the sleeves of their robes rolled up, you can easily identify them (one of the few cases in which global warming might come in handy). However, their distinctive

eaters during the phase in which the NIAC is ongoing. As previously highlighted, this is only the case during the time around the Battle of Hogwarts. During that time, the death eaters exert control over the wizarding world as the Minister of Magic, Pius Thicknesse, is acting based on their will (thanks to a lovingly imposed *Imperius* curse). They *de facto* control the wizarding government and can therefore be considered the "governing party". The death eaters and Voldemort will therefore in this case be like the national government—please let that sink in for a while.

3.3.4   And What About the Order of the Phoenix?

Now what does this mean for the Order of the Phoenix members and the teachers of Hogwarts who fought in the Battle of Hogwarts. Just to recap, the Order of the Phoenix is a secret society founded by Professor Dumbledore to fight against Voldemort and the death eaters after the return of Voldemort to Britain and during the First Wizarding War. Back then, many members of the Order died fighting against Voldemort.[59] After the return of Voldemort, the Order was reconvened within an hour.[60] Its members were thereafter involved in the battle at the Ministry of Magic in the Department of Mysteries among others.

   After Voldemort took over control of the Ministry, the Order of the Phoenix led the underground resistance. They participated in the radio program Potterwatch and encouraged people to protect Muggles and Muggle-borns alike. During this phase, as we had mentioned before, there was no armed conflict and therefore no need to assess the status of the members of the Order. This changed during the Battle of Hogwarts. Let's take a closer look: we are in a NIAC, there is therefore no combatant status.[61] This leaves the option of them being considered civilians directly participating in hostilities or even members of an armed group with a continuous combat function (remember, this is important to understand for how long they all lose their protection). Of course, other options might come to mind such as "freedom fighters" or "terrorists". But please bear in mind that these are ways to describe how you feel about people participating in a conflict, not legal classifications.[62] However strong you feel about it, does not change the fact that you can't make up additional categories as you go along. Well, unless you are a judge or well renowned legal scholar. Then you actually can. But a book introducing international law through the

---

sign plays no role in qualifying as combatants because we are not dealing with an international but a NIAC where this status does not exist (otherwise, this would have been a great case to make). The death eaters never knew the identities of the fellow death eaters. .

[59] This included the members of the original Order of the Phoenix Marlene McKinnon, Benjy Fenwick, Edgar Bones, Caradoc Dearborn, Gideon Prewett, Dorcas Meadows and Harry's parents. More on this in: Rowling (2003), Chapter 5: The Order of the Phoenix.

[60] Rowling (2003), Chapter 5: The Order of the Phoenix.

[61] More details on why there are no combatants in NIAC: Solis (2010), p. 190.

[62] More on this in: Cameron and Chetail (2013), p. 425.

lens of Harry Potter literature might not be the ideal place for this. At least in this edition.

To test whether the members of the Order of the Phoenix (think Lupin, Tonks and the Weasley parents—we will take the short form "Order" from here on to save space) were directly participating in hostilities, we'll have to test the three core elements. Let's recap, we need to reach the threshold of harm, there has to be a direct causal link between the act of the members of the Order and the harm inflicted and there needs to be a belligerent nexus.[63]

The members of the Order certainly crossed the threshold of harm. They killed numerous death eaters (think about Molly Weasley ending the shrieks of Bellatrix Lestrange). In many cases, there was a direct causal link between the acts and the harm inflicted (say the spell, swing the wand, people drop dead). Finally, there is also the belligerent nexus. And yes, that is also quite an easy one. The acts of the members of the Order were clearly intended to harm the death eaters and benefit the Order and Hogwarts.

As we can see, the members of the Order are civilians directly participating in hostilities. The same goes for those defending Hogwarts (for one example, just take the teachers, meaning of course those defending Hogwarts, not the Carrow siblings who went to join their master, Voldemort). Let's now assess if they are also members of an armed group with a continuous combat function. Just as a reminder, this is relevant as it means that they could be lawfully targeted by the Ministry of Magic forces even when they are not actively fighting.

For this, we'll have to take a closer look at the Order and the broader group that was fighting during the Battle of Hogwarts. Given that they were all only involved in one major battle, their participation in hostilities cannot be categorized as regular in any way. Yes, they also tried to rally the resistance (e.g., Hagrid trying to befriend the giants) but there was no active fighting going on between the Order and the death eaters. Looking back at our example of "farmer by day, fighter by night"—there was not even a good night's sleep between their regular activities and fighting against the death eaters. The members of the Order of the Phoenix, the Hogwarts teachers (and yes, let's not forget all the other volunteers who fought alongside the Order) were civilians directly participating in hostilities. This means they lost their protection as civilians for the duration of their direct participation in hostilities but afterwards regained this protection.[64] Among those who fought were also members of Dumbledore's Army. For them, not only the question of whether they were directly participating in hostilities is important. It is, instead, also a question of whether they would be considered child soldiers. If you don't remember who they are, don't worry. A description will follow in the next section.

---

[63] To recap, these three criteria were previously explained in Sect. 3.3.2.

[64] More on this in Cameron and Chetail (2013), p. 387.

3.4 Are the Members of Dumbledore's Army Child Soldiers?

As Molly Weasley continued to point out to Ginny right before the Battle of Hogwarts, Ginny was still considered as "under-age" and Bill requested everyone under-age to leave as this were the right thing to do.[65] While I agree with this gut feeling, the underlying question is: what does the law say about a bunch of students taking up arms, or better, wands, to fight Voldemort. Thankfully, law is there to help and we can take a look at the law on child soldiers to better understand what is lawful and who might have violated legal requirements.

3.4.1 How Does Law Define Child Soldiers?

There are of course several different definitions for child soldiers. Let us look at the most relevant definitions to better understand what we are talking about. Based on Art. 38 of the UN Convention on the Rights of the Child, states have to ensure that those under 15 years old are not taking direct part in hostilities (Art. 38 (2)) and have to refrain from recruiting them into their armed forces (Art. 38 (3)).[66] The Optional Protocol on the Involvement of Children in Armed Conflict has even stricter rules. It states that members of the armed forces should not take direct part in hostilities if they are under 18 years old (Art. 1) or armed forces compulsory recruit those under 18 (Art. 2). It also states that armed groups should not recruit or use those under 18 in hostilities (Art. 4 (1)) and that states should "take all feasible measures to prevent such recruitment and use, including the adoption of legal measures necessary to prohibit and criminalize such practices" (Art. 4 (2)).

Beyond these two regulations, there are also the provisions in AP I (for IAC) and AP II (for NIAC), stating that states have to refrain from recruiting anyone under the age of 15 to their armed forces or allowing them to take direct part in hostilities. (Art. 77 (2) AP I and Art. 4 (3) c AP II).[67]

Then—to make life even more complicated—there is also the Rome Statute of the ICC. Art. 8 makes conscripting or enlisting children under the age of 15 or their use to directly participate in hostilities a war crime in both IAC and NIAC.

Now what do we make of all of this? As we learned initially, it depends on what the state has signed and ratified. Given the principle of state sovereignty, international obligations only become relevant for the states in these cases (with certain exceptions, I know).[68] So, it will depend on whether the Ministry of Magic has ratified any of these treaties. We'll assume not (given the Statute of Secrecy) but let's

---

[65]Rowling (2007), Chapter 30: The Sacking of Severus Snape.

[66]Convention on the Rights of the Child, GA resolution 44/25, https://www.ohchr.org/en/professionalinterest/pages/crc.aspx. Accessed 12 December 2022.

[67]More details on this in Kälin and Künzli (2010), pp. 426 ff.

[68]More details on this in Kälin and Künzli (2010), p. 36.

still look at whether the members of Dumbledore's Army would qualify in either case.

3.4.2   What Does This Mean for Dumbledore's Army?

Before applying international law to this situation, let's first try to understand what Dumbledore's Army was. As a response to Dolores Umbridge taking over Defense Against the Dark Arts and thereby ridding the subject of any real-life applicability, Hermione came up with the idea that Harry should pass on his knowledge about fighting dark wizards and teach his fellow classmates the essential spells to allow them to protect themselves. When assessing whether Dumbledore's Army is indeed a group of child soldiers, there are two different phases which have to be differentiated. The first phase is the phase when Harry is teaching the group of students during his 5th year at Hogwarts. The second phase is when Hogwarts fell under the control of Voldemort sympathizers in the year leading up to the Battle of Hogwarts. As an important side note—the name Dumbledore's Army derived from the first suggestion by Cho Chang of naming it Defence Association and Ginny Weasley's idea to make the letters DA stand for Dumbledore's Army as this would be the Ministry of Magic's worst fear. It was, however, not intended for an armed conflict.[69]

3.4.2.1 Dumbledore's Army During Harry's 5th Year at Hogwarts
Dumbledore's Army was founded by twenty-eight members. During the first phase, the group was meeting to practice spells such as the Disarming Charm, the Impediment Jinx, the Reductor Curse, the Stunning Spell, the Shield Charm and the Patronus Charm. Their goal was to both prepare to protect themselves in a world in which Voldemort had returned and the death eaters were on the rise, as well as for passing the O.W.L. exams, which also included a practical part for which the textbook course by Professor Umbridge would have left them utterly unprepared. The group was disbanded when Umbridge became aware of the group's existence due to a group member's betrayal.[70]

While this put an end to the practice sessions of Dumbledore's Army, Dumbledore's Army survived until the Battle in the Ministry of Magic during which Harry, Ron, Hermione, Neville, Luna and Ginny, all members of Dumbledore's Army, fought the death eaters alongside the members of the Order of the Phoenix.

But does this mean that this fight in the Ministry of Magic might make the six members of Dumbledore's Army child soldiers? Yes, there were several members of the Order of the Phoenix, the death eaters and the Aurors involved. Yet, they were not fighting in an armed conflict (as highlighted before). They were therefore also

---

[69]Rowling (2003), Chapter 18: Dumbledore's Army.

[70]More on this in: Rowling (2003), Chapter 27: The Centaur and the Sneak.

not recruited by an armed group or taking direct part in hostilities. They were therefore not child soldiers during Harry's 5th year at Hogwarts. Instead, they were more like a sports club which members ended up in an unfortunate situation, rather than child soldiers.

3.4.2.2 Dumbledore's Army Leading Up to the Battle of Hogwarts

The second phase of the group's activities began when the Ministry of Magic fell under the control of Voldemort and his death eaters. Professor Snape became headmaster of Hogwarts and the death eaters Alecto and Amycus Carrow were appointed professors. Neville Longbottom, Luna Lovegood and Ginny Weasley revived Dumbledore's Army.[71] They painted slogans on the wall and acted against the Headmaster and the Carrows. When it came to the Battle of Hogwarts, members of Dumbledore's Army fought alongside the Order of the Phoenix, teachers of Hogwarts and some Hogsmeade shopkeepers against the death eaters. But were they child soldiers during this phase?

As we had established, there was a NIAC going on during the time of the Battle of Hogwarts. First the critical age question. As identified before, there are different minimum ages that are held up based on international law. The lowest of these is 15. As in the wizarding world 17 is the legal age, let's assume that any voluntary modification of that minimum age requirement would only have been to change it from 15 to 17, but not 18 years of age. Were there any students below the age of 17 or even below the age of 15 involved in the Battle of Hogwarts? Sadly, the answer is yes. Just remember the Colin Creevey who entered the fight despite only being 16 years old and thus being considered underage in the wizarding world (given that age limit of 17 for everything else, let's assume it also applies for any potential regulation of child soldiers).[72]

Yet, does this automatically mean that child soldiers were used by the opposition (meaning the Order and all others defending Hogwarts)? Not really. As we had seen in the texts of the different regulations, it is required that the armed forces or armed group recruit those underage or allow them to take direct part in hostilities.[73] In the Battle of Hogwarts, those defending Hogwarts had explicitly aimed to send all of those underage into safety through the Room of Requirement. They therefore neither recruited the underage members of Dumbledore's Army for the battle, nor did they endorse their direct partaking in hostilities.

So no, the members of Dumbledore's Army were not legally child soldiers, even though a few of them managed to join the fight against the death eaters. In fact, this is one of the few moments in which the Carrow siblings actually did something right by trying to disband Dumbledore's Army. While their intention (very likely) was not to prevent a violation of regulation against child soldiers, their actions could be

---

[71] Rowling (2007), Chapter 29: The Lost Diadem.

[72] Rowling (2007), Chapter 32: The Elder Wand.

[73] In case you have forgotten this already, go back to Sect. 3.4.1.

construed as trying to ensure that no underage wizards join the fight against the death eaters.

3.5   What if the Hogwarts Suits of Armor Had Gone Rogue?

In the Battle of Hogwarts, Professor McGonagall has a real bad-ass moment and uses the incantation *Piertotum Locomotor* to bring the previously inanimate and unmoving Hogwarts suits of armor and statues to life. They then move to fight in the final battle and protect Hogwarts.

Once the suits of armor and statues start moving towards the death eaters, every legal scholar (when done cheering for McGonagall's ingenious move) of course has to ask: who controls their acts and bears responsibility for their actions? What if they had decided to join forces with the death eaters?

Luckily, there is a way to start answering these important questions. To do so, we do, however, first need to take a look at the most similar scenario: autonomous weapon systems (AWS). Yes, you read correctly. For those of you who don't know what autonomous weapon systems are, think Terminator, meaning killer robots—just in real, but neither looking for Sarah Connor nor going rogue in any other way (not even talking about Artificial Intelligence becoming sentient and deciding the planet would be better off without humans). Of course, lawyers have more sophisticated ways of explaining this to us.

3.5.1   Autonomous Weapon Systems (AWS)

As society is getting more and more used to autonomous systems (yes, they even have autonomous cars now, think about how much Mr. Weasley would love that), one phenomenon is leading to lots of discussions: AWS.[74] The critical difference to understand is that between automatic systems, automated systems and autonomous ones (if I am close to losing your attention, bear with me, we'll soon be back to our *Piertotum Locomotor* moment). Automatic systems don't make any decisions, they just react to triggers. A simple example is a mechanical thermostat that activates the aircon once a certain temperature threshold is exceeded.[75] Automated systems are a bit more sophisticated. They function rules-based. To stick with Scharre's thermostat example—the equivalent would be a digital programmable thermostat that can turn on the aircon depending on temperature, day and time.[76] Autonomous machines can make decisions based on information they process, they don't only react to triggers.[77] They are goal-oriented but flexible in how to achieve them, such as

---

[74]For a general introduction of AWS: Scharre (2018).

[75]ibid., 31.

[76]ibid.

[77]Marra and McNeil (2013), pp. 15–18; Crootof (2015), p. 1855.

self-driving cars.[78] We will focus on the last category, the autonomous machines. There are three different levels of human involvement with these machines: semiautonomous operations (with a human in the loop), supervised autonomous operations (with a human on the loop) and fully autonomous operations (with a human out of the loop). If you want to learn more about this, read Scharre's book. Let us take the example of de-gnoming. Assume for a minute that this were a problem Muggles had to face, not only witches and wizards. As you know, people tend to be lazy and invent tools for everything they can (just think about the banana slicer for one second before you disagree). Now, imagine someone had invented an autonomous de-gnoming bot. If a person still had to make decisions in the de-gnoming process (e.g., which method of de-gnoming to choose or whether to continue), this would be a human in the loop situation. If the person were purely able to supervise what the bot was doing but didn't have to intervene unless choosing to, this would be a human on the loop situation. The last scenario—human out of the loop—is if the person were sitting inside the Borrow, gave the bot the overall instruction to go "de-gnom" and the bot went and did this all by itself while the person had some butterbeer. For us, the category of fully autonomous operations will—quite obviously—be most interesting.

AWS—meaning the ones that people fear as "killer robots"[79] are considered fully autonomous, without having a human in the loop. They can take decisions based on information they process and are not guided in their actions by a human superior.

But what if AWS don't do as they were supposed to? What if based on their processing of data, they decide to hurt the wrong side or even switch sides? Is that possible and if so, who would be to blame for any resulting harm?

This is a question that lawyers and politicians love to debate but which has not yet been resolved. Lawyers and politicians keep on highlighting that IHL applies to AWS and their development just as with any other weapon system. Great, so what does this mean for us now? Two questions will be particularly interesting when considering the statues and suits of armor of Hogwarts (for all other questions, I'll happily point you to my book on this topic in the hopes of boosting sales).[80] First, we want to understand what those developing AWS must bear in mind to make sure they comply with IHL. Second, we want to know who is responsible if AWS are not doing what they were supposed to do.

Let's start with the first question. What do you have to bear in mind should you ever decide to develop an AWS. If that should be the case, make sure to read Art. 36 AP I before doing so.

Art. 36 AP I

---

[78] Scharre (2018), p. 31.

[79] A fascinating video developed by those lobbying for a ban on "killer robots" is the Slaughterbots video: https://www.youtube.com/watch?v=9CO6M2HsoIA.

[80] For more background reading (in case you find this topic as fascinating as I do), check out the following: Renz (2020), Crootof and Renz (2017), and Crootof (2015).

In the study, development, acquisition or adoption of a new weapon, means or method of warfare, a High Contracting Party is under an obligation to determine whether its employment would, in some or all circumstances, be prohibited by this Protocol or by any other rule of international law applicable to the High Contracting Party.

Now that we have read it—what does Art. 36 AP I mean for your future endeavors? As you can see, the obligation to ensure that everything is in accordance with international law is directed to the "High Contracting Party". Sounds like you are off the hook. If you are working for a government, the government would have to make sure that it properly tests the new weapon system and ensures that no violations of international law can occur. If you develop this system yourself, there might be consequences under national criminal law to fear—but no direct obligation under international law (remember, you are not a state).[81]

The second question is who is responsible in case something goes wrong. I'll pause for a second to let you think whether this rings a bell. Yes, indeed (five points to those who remember)—we are in the territory of state responsibility and will have to check again whether the government has followed its obligations in case it deploys an AWS and something goes wrong.[82] But what if it was not the fault of the government but an individual who decided to start using AWS? Imagine a more tech-savvy Aunt Marge developing an AWS and letting it roam freely in her neighborhood. Well, that would indeed be more difficult. We would have to test whether the government could have done anything to prevent it (only possible if government employees knew or should have known that Aunt Marge developed the AWS) and we can hold Aunt Marge accountable under national criminal and civil law. Without going into the details, this basically means that the court in Britain could decide whether she violated any British laws by letting AWS roam freely in the neighborhood and she would quite likely be held accountable for it under national criminal and civil law.

3.5.2   The Hogwarts Suits of Armor and Statues as AWS

What does all of this mean for the Hogwarts suits of armor and the statues? Let's first try to understand whether they could be considered AWS. When McGonagall uses the spell *Piertotum Locomotor* she shouts at the statues and suits of armor: "Hogwarts is threatened!" and "Man the boundaries, protect us, do your duty to our school!"[83] Afterwards, we only hear stories about the statues and suits of armor

---

[81] For more on the obligations under Art. 36 AP I related to AWS: McClelland (2003) and Boulanin (2015).

[82] More on this fascinating subject in this incredibly well-written book: Renz (2020).

[83] Rowling (2007), Chapter 30: The Sacking of Severus Snape.

defending the castle. If we think back to the distinctions between a human in the loop, human on the loop or human out of the loop this is a clear-cut case. Prof. McGonagall is exerting no control whatsoever over the specific acts of the statues and suits of armor. She gave them an order on what the overall objective was, but every tactical decision about what to do next is fully up to the suits of armor and statues themselves. Under our interpretation, they would therefore qualify as fully autonomous weapon systems.[84]

3.5.3   What if the Suits of Armor or Statues Had Gone Rogue?

Now let's imagine some of the suits of armor had gone rogue. Would that have been possible you might ask. Well, just consider the craziness that is going on around you. Your computer deciding not to start, Siri misunderstanding everything you try to tell her. Add magic to that mix and tell me what is or is not possible.

First, we'll have to understand whether anyone has violated Art. 36 AP I and did not sufficiently test them prior to their deployment. The difficulty is that we don't know who developed the suits of armor and statues. Let's assume, for arguments sake, that they date back to the time of the Hogwarts' founders. Whoever among them had his or her hands in their development will be long gone and difficult to hold accountable.

This leaves us with the second option: state responsibility. As we have previously established, the government was controlled by those loyal to Voldemort during the Battle of Hogwarts. But does it matter that Prof. McGonagall—who said the spell that ordered them to defend Hogwarts—is a teacher at Hogwarts?

Let's first try to understand the status of Hogwarts—public or private school? We don't really have that level of visibility when it comes to Hogwarts. In some instances it seems as though Hogwarts is a private school, given the level of autonomy that Dumbledore enjoys. In other instances, there is heavy government involvement. This includes not only Umbridge's role as Inquisitor but also the role of the Board of Governors. The 12 witches and wizards of the Board of Governors have the right to inspect and even shut down the school. Yet, this still does not fully answer our question. Now looking at the phase during which the statues were awoken by Prof. McGonagall, this question is a bit easier to answer: After Voldemort took over the Ministry of Magic, the death eaters also seized control over Hogwarts, instated themselves as professors (e.g., our lovely Carrows) and made enrollment mandatory. So yes, in this very year we can consider Hogwarts very much a public school. But does this mean that the state—in this case the death eater led government—is responsible for the act of Prof. McGonagall?

---

[84]More details on how this already exists and is way more than drones: Scharre (2018).

As we had discussed earlier, state responsibility can arise from acts and omissions (doing something wrong or not preventing something wrong from happening).[85] We will not be easily able to qualify Prof. McGonagall as a state official (given her obvious disconnect with the state and lack of a role in its government) but was there an omission by any state officials who could have prevented her from unleashing the statues? Let's be honest—if they could have, they would, given the state of things at that point. So while it was clearly not in the interest of the government to see the statues defend Hogwarts, there seems to have been limited things they could have done to prevent this from happening. And as they did all they could, there is no state responsibility for omission.

The only option to achieve accountability would therefore be under national wizarding law in case this has any similar regulations as Muggle law (treating this in similar way was you would situations in which a pet hurts someone).

3.6   Are the Dementors the Equivalent to Private Military and Security Contractors?

We talked about the dementors earlier—the lovely band of semi-ghosts that literally suck the soul out of those they are guarding, chasing or just happen to stumble across in a bad moment. Yet, until the wizarding world came to its senses, the dementors were guarding the wizarding prison Azkaban. The urge to outsource the role of guards in prisons to a non-governmental entity is something that should feel very familiar to many among us. The same is done with many prisons where private security contractors take over guard duties and more. But are there similarities? And if so, is there any way to regulate what the private security contractors—or in our case dementors—are allowed to do?

3.6.1   Private Military and Security Contractors

Private security contractors take over many of the roles that the government cannot or does not want to take on, such as the guarding of prisons. They also guard embassies or work for private companies, such as guarding their sites in complex environments (euphemism meaning conflict zone). Just think of an oil field in Iraq as one of the typical examples.[86] When you live in a country such as the Philippines, you will see private security guards in front of every shopping mall. They are quite easy to spot—basically any person that is not from the military/police/any other governmental entity but that is standing in front of a building they guard or close to a

---

[85] In case you have forgotten about the basic rules of state responsibility (no worries if you did, you are not confounded, it has just been a lot to take in), please check out Sect. 2.2.1 again.

[86] If you want to learn more about the history of the private security industry, I can highly recommend the following books: McFate (2014) and Singer (2007).

person they are protecting. There are, as always, many debates about terminology and one term frequently used to describe these actors is private military and security companies (PMSCs) as it covers not only the provision of security services, but also that of military services.[87] Again, for those interested in the topic, I'd like to shamelessly advertise a brilliant book on this topic as well as a few fascinating articles.[88]

There are certain rules that highlight what these contractors are allowed to do (yes, this is the case, even though there are many claims to the contrary).[89] There are three different levels of regulation concerning PMSCs:

- international and regional regulatory efforts,
- self-regulatory and voluntary initiatives, and
- national regulation.

On the international and regional level, the most important conventions are the UN Mercenary Convention and the Organization of African Unity (OAU) Convention. A key problem with the UN Mercenary Convention is the definition of mercenaries in Art. 1, which is based on Art. 47 AP I. A focus of this definition is on the intent of the potential mercenary.[90] This complicates subsuming anyone under this category as it is almost impossible to prove financial gain as the sole or predominant motivation.[91] Without the magical power of *legilimency* (reading someone's mind, remember, Harry tried to shield himself against this special power of Voldemort's without much success), imagine you have to figure out what the true motivation of a person you just met really is. Other problems boil down to the nature of the business, relying on subcontractors and claiming to operate with self-defense as business model.[92] We won't need to go into more details here, but just to give you a sense of how likely it is that anyone will classify as a mercenary under the Mercenary Convention, there is an infamous quote that states: "any mercenary who cannot exclude himself from this definition deserves to be shot – and his lawyer with him!"[93] Even if anyone were considered a mercenary, it hardly matters as only 37 states have ratified this Convention, none of them being a state

---

[87] I will spare you the debate about whether PMSCs are mercenaries—but in case you can't resist, here you find further info on this intricate subject: Renz (2017), pp. 309 ff.; Avant (2004); Singer (2004), p. 529; Percy (2007), p. 379.

[88] Renz (2017, 2020).

[89] Tiefer (2009), p. 745; Whitten (2012), p. 503.

[90] Arguing that this psychological element should not play a role in IHL: Cassese (1980), p. 25. For a differing view: Taulbee (1985), pp. 339, 352. For a thorough discussion of the requirements set forth in Art. 47 AP I: Maaß (1990), pp. 100–123.

[91] Singer (2004), p. 529; Percy (2007), p. 379; Elsea (2010), p. 7.

[92] de Wolf (2006), p. 323; Avant (2004), p. 20; Wyttenbach (2014), p. 434; Gaston (2008), p. 233. Analyzing the mercenary definition: Mancini et al. (2011), p. 339; Sassòli (2013), p. 118.

[93] Percy (2012), p. 945 referring to the original quote by Geoffrey Best.

that actually leads in contracting PMSCs.[94] The OAU Convention faces very similar challenges as it also bases its rules on the definition of Art. 47 AP I. The UN has attempted to regulate PMSCs in a Convention.[95] To continue the process to establish a binding international treaty on PMSCs, the UN even set up a working group, aptly titled the "Open-ended intergovernmental working group to consider the possibility of elaborating an international regulatory framework on the regulation, monitoring and oversight of the activities of private military and security companies."[96] If this does not scream commitment to regulate, what does. Also, if there is any group that Percy Weasley with his love for cauldron regulation certainly would love to join, this seems to be it.

Before we leave the murky waters of international law and do a quick detour to voluntary and self-regulatory initiatives, one word of caution. If you get as fascinated by this subject as I am, you'll read a lot about PMSCs operating in legal grey areas. To some degree that is true, to some degree it is not. PMSC employees are subject to legal norms just as all other people are. The rules of IHL apply to them just as they apply to any other person not involved in security services, such as Mr. Dursley. Though, in all honesty, it is more likely that PMSC employees end up in a situation in which IHL actually applies.

Now let's move on to self-regulation and voluntary initiatives. Yes, they are not as good as international law. But they can come in quite handy. Regulation of PMSCs is largely driven by self-regulation and voluntary initiatives that are not legally binding but shape industry practices.[97] The key documents that you'll need to know as a diligent lawyer are the Montreux Document on pertinent international legal obligations and good practices for States related to operations of private military and security companies during armed conflict (Montreux Document) as well as the International Code of Conduct (ICoC). The Montreux Document is the result of an initiative by the Swiss Federal Department of Foreign Affairs as well as

---

[94] UN Treaty Collection. Status of the Mercenary Convention. https://treaties.un.org/Pages/ViewDetails.aspx?src=IND&mtdsg_no=XVIII-6&chapter=18&clang=_en.

[95] More on the UN Working Group on the Use of Mercenarism as a Means of Violating Human Rights and Impeding the Exercise of the Right of Peoples to Self-Determination (yes, that's a mouth full—try repeating that 5 times) that had its mandate expanded in 2008 to also include PMSCs in the following UN Documents: UN Commission on Human Rights, The Use of Mercenaries as a Means of Violating Human Rights and Impeding the Exercise of the Right of Peoples to Self-determination, 7 April 2005, UN Doc. E/CN.4/RES/2005/2; UN HRC, Mandate of the Working Group on the Use of Mercenaries as a Means of Violating Human Rights and Impeding the Exercise of the Right of Peoples to Self-determination, 28 March 2008, UN Doc. A/HRC/RES/7/21. The Draft Convention can be found in the Annex of: UN HRC, Report of the Working Group on the Use of Mercenaries as a Means of Violating Human Rights and Impeding the Exercise of the Right of Peoples to Self-determination, 2 July 2010, UN Doc. A/HRC/15/25.

[96] UN HRC, Open-ended Intergovernmental Working Group to Consider the Possibility of Elaborating an International Regulatory Framework on the Regulation, Monitoring and Oversight of the Activities of Private Military and Security Companies, 1 October 2010, UN Doc. A/HRC/RES/15/26.

[97] Richemond-Barak (2014), pp. 776–777.

the ICRC. It provides guidance for states in how to regulate PMSCs.[98] The ICoC is the result of a multi-stakeholder initiative (MSI) initiative by Switzerland.[99] The goal of the initiative was to formulate human rights responsibilities of PMSCs as well as establish international principles and standards.[100] PMSCs can apply to become members of the ICoC Association (ICoCA). For this to be possible, they have to be certified to an industry standard recognized by the ICoCA board, such as PSC.1 standard, the ISO28007 standard or the ISO 18788 standard. What this means—for the non-lawyers among you, is that if you were to run a PMSC you have to prove that you are for example vetting your employees and have the needed policies in place in case of any incidents.[101] Governments often times require companies they hire to be a member of ICoCA, which in turn means that the PMSC needs to be certified to certain standards.

Beyond all of this, there is also national regulation but I will spare you from going into the depths of these questions as well.[102] To summarize all that you have just read: yes, there are many private security companies and no, their work is neither illegal nor completely unregulated. There are, however, many blind spots in their regulation. Now let's try to understand whether the dementors could be considered private security contractors.

3.6.2   Comparison to the Role of Dementors in Azkaban

The definition of a PMSC is (based on the Montreux Document we looked at before):

> **Montreux Document**
> PMSCs are private business entities that provide military and/or security services, irrespective of how they describe themselves. Military and security services include, in particular, armed guarding and protection of persons and objects, such as convoys, buildings and other places; maintenance and operation of weapons systems; prisoner detention; and advice to or training of local forces and security personnel.

---

[98] Montreux Document on pertinent international legal obligations and good practices for States related to operations of private military and security companies during armed conflicts, https://www.montreuxdocument.org/pdf/document/en.pdf.

[99] Wyttenbach (2014), p. 440.

[100] Percy (2012), p. 954.

[101] More on the issue of industry standards and voluntary regulation in: DeWinter-Schmitt (2016), pp. 258–259; Renz (2020), pp. 29 ff.

[102] In case you are looking for more insights on this, please check out the following ingenious book: Renz (2020), pp. 33 ff.

Now, does this sound like the dementors? First of all, what are dementors? Well, they are definitely not humans but some other type of magical being. Yet what exactly remains difficult to determine. They appear to be owned by no one. Instead, they seem to follow orders or agreements with witches and wizards, at least sometimes.

Now back to our question on whether they are PMSCs. Let's start from the type of services they offer: yes, they are definitely in charge of prisoner detention. Their "service" therefore falls under the definition of military and security services. Yet, the challenge will be on whether the dementors are a "private business entity". One could argue that the dementors are providing their services in exchange for access to human souls, a central requirement for them. This might seem like a business-like relationship between the Ministry of Magic and the dementors. While we don't know about any official contracts, some types of agreements seem to exist. At least there are indications of this when the dementors are stationed around Hogwarts and have clear rules on what they are allowed or not allowed to do.

To understand the role of the dementors in Azkaban, it is essential to gain a brief understanding of their role. Before the International Statute of Secrecy was imposed in 1692, there were small wizarding prisons across the country. Those were now considered security risks as the attempts by witches and wizards to break free were frequently accompanied with loud noises, light shows or smells. It was then decided to leverage Azkaban—as this is where the dementors were living—given that they would be the ideal guards. One concern, though, was that many prisoners were going insane or died of despair. While there was a moment where alternatives were explored, the fear was that the dementors would start to roam free if they did not have a constant supply of new souls.[103]

This clearly highlights that the reliance on the dementors is less a question of whether they were engaged as private security contractors—the equivalent to private security companies guarding prisons—and more a question of state-sanctioned torture of prisoners, an issue we will tackle later in this book.

The special relationship with the Ministry of Magic certainly ended when Voldemort returned and went into the open after the battle in the Ministry of Magic.[104] Yes, you will ask what happened to the dementors. I do not know, if you find out, please let me know.

But what does this mean in terms of regulating the dementors? Frankly, the regulation of PMSC in the Muggle world will be of limited use in this case, we will need to look beyond this at anti-torture regulation[105] and the regulation of dangerous creatures (a subject to be covered in a future volume but not in this particular book). So, unfortunately for Percy Weasley, no Open-ended intergovernmental working group to consider the possibility of elaborating an international

---

[103] For the full background please refer to: Rowling (2015), Azkaban.

[104] Rowling (2015), Azkaban.

[105] On the question whether reliance on dementors is torture the below chapter will be of interest: Sect. 4.5.2.

regulatory framework on the regulation, monitoring and oversight of the activities of dementors any time soon.

3.7   Could the Scourers Be Considered Mercenaries?

3.7.1   What Are Mercenaries?

Mercenaries, yes, that will ring a bell. We just talked about mercenaries in our last section. Let's look back at that. As you have learned, Art. 47 AP defines mercenaries for us.

Art. 47 AP I

1. A mercenary shall not have the right to be a combatant or a prisoner of war.
2. A mercenary is any person who:
   (a) is specially recruited locally or abroad in order to fight in an armed conflict;
   (b) does, in fact, take a direct part in the hostilities;
   (c) is motivated to take part in the hostilities essentially by the desire for private gain and, in fact, is promised, by or on behalf of a Party to the conflict, material compensation substantially in excess of that promised or paid to combatants of similar ranks and functions in the armed forces of that Party;
   (d) is neither a national of a Party to the conflict nor a resident of territory controlled by a Party to the conflict;
   (e) is not a member of the armed forces of a Party to the conflict; and
   (f) has not been sent by a State which is not a Party to the conflict on official duty as a member of its armed forces.

If you struggle connecting this definition to anything you've heard in your history lessons, let me help you out. Mercenaries are sometimes described as the second oldest profession in the world.[106] They were active throughout history, with famous mercenaries being the Swiss mercenaries serving armies all across Europe in the sixteenth and seventeenth century as well as the German *Landsknechte* as major players. Beyond that think British East India Company and Dutch East India Trading Company—the army of the British East India Company alone encompassed 150,000 soldiers and 122 ships.[107] But mercenary activity is not limited to these far-gone times. There was an increase in the 1950s and 1960s, driven by national liberation movements in the wake of decolonization. The end of the Cold War meant that the great powers were less interested in military intervention and downsized their

---

[106]Renz (2020), pp. 19 ff.

[107]More on this fascinating topic in: Singer (2007), pp. 26 ff; Thomson (1994), p. 24; McFate (2014), pp. 50–51.

military. Military contractors such as Executive Outcomes, a South African company, were conducting military operations during civil wars such as in Angola and Sierra Leone.[108] Today, one of the best-known mercenaries groups is the Russian Wagner group that has acted as guns-for-hire across Central African Republic, Syria, Ukraine and Yemen.[109]

But what does all of this mean? As we had discussed earlier, there is anti-mercenary regulation which applies to mercenaries falling under the above definition.[110] Based on the UN Mercenary Convention, states are forbidden from recruiting, using, financing and training mercenaries. Which basically makes them unemployed. But why are mercenaries not gone then, you might ask. Well, only few states have signed and ratified the UN Mercenary Convention, which means that for all other states, it is still ok to recruit, use, finance and train mercenaries.[111] Again, this is the nature of international law—aside from a few basic principles, it only applies to the extent that states sign up to it (if this seems irritating, go back to the first chapters looking into state sovereignty).

Now, the two relevant questions are whether mercenaries exist in the wizarding world and if so, whether they are regulated in any way?

3.7.2   Scourers as the Wizarding World's Mercenaries?

As not all of you might know who the Scourers are, let's do a quick detour first to understand what we are talking about. The Scourers were an unscrupulous band of wizards of many foreign nationalities, roaming around North America. They were the result of the small, scattered and secretive wizarding community in North America, in which no distinct law enforcement mechanism had evolved. The Scourers were a brutal task force which hunted down known criminals and also others who might be worth some gold. As is the risk with such a profession, the Scourers were reported to have become increasingly corrupt. They enjoyed torture and bloodshed and trafficked fellow wizards. MACUSA put the Scourers on trial and executed those convicted of murder, wizard-trafficking, torture and many other acts of cruelty.[112]

---

[108]More on this history: Hasian (2011), pp. 273–274; Hoover (1977), p. 341; Spear (2006), pp. 11–13, 29–30; Avant (2005); McFate (2014), p. 14.

[109]More details on the Wagner Group and their political ties: Rondeaux (2019). As I promised that this is a non-political piece of work, we will let the domestic dynamics linked to Wagner group out of scope.

[110]If you want to take a look at the regulation again, please refer back to Sect. 3.6.1.

[111]If you want to know the exact number of how many states have signed and ratified the UN Mercenary Convention, look here in the UN Treaty Collection (a treasure trove of information about all the UN treaties, who signed them, who ratified them): https://treaties.un.org/Pages/ViewDetails.aspx?src=IND&mtdsg_no=XVIII-6&chapter=18&clang=_en.

[112]Rowling (2016).

Well, they don't sound like a group of people you'd like to meet. But would they qualify as mercenaries? Let's take a look at the definition. To be considered mercenaries, they would need to be recruited to fight in an armed conflict and take direct part in hostilities. While they were certainly doing their fair share of fighting, there is no known record of them being actively involved in any type of armed conflict. This might be due to a lack of reliable records covering these early years of wizarding history in North America. Yet, as we have to stick to the facts, we have to assume that they were indeed not recruited to fight in any armed conflict. This means that the scourers do not meet the criteria for mercenaries under Art. 47 AP I.

So the answer is simple: there are no known mercenaries in the wizarding world—or they are just extremely good at their job and are hiding their activities better than their Muggle counterparts.

References

Akande D (2010) Clearing the fog of war? The ICRC's interpretive guidance on direct participation in hostilities. Int Comp Law Q 59:180–192

Akande D (2012) Classification of armed conflicts: relevant legal concepts. In: Wilmshurst E (ed) International law and the classification of conflicts. Oxford University Press, Oxford, pp 32–79

Allansson M, Melander E, Themnér L (2017) Organized violence, 1989-2016. J Peace Res 54:574–587

Avant D (2004) Mercenaries. Foreign Policy 143:20–28

Avant D (2005) The market for force: the consequences of privatizing security. Cambridge University Press, Cambridge

Bernard V (2014) Delineating the boundaries of violence. Int Rev Red Cros 96:5–11

Boulanin V (2015) Implementing Article 26 weapon reviews in the light of increasing autonomy in weapon systems. SIPRI insights on peace and security 2015/1

Cameron L, Chetail V (2013) Privatizing war: private military and security companies under public international law. Cambridge University Press, New York

Cassese A (1980) Mercenaries: lawful combatants or war criminals? Zeitschrift für ausländisches öffentliches Recht und Völkerrecht 40:1–30

Cassese A (2014) Current challenges to international humanitarian law. In: Clapham A, Gaeta P (eds) . Oxford University Press, Oxford

Crawford E (2015) Identifying the enemy: civilian participation in armed conflict. Oxford University Press, New York

Crootof R (2015) The killer robots are here: legal and policy implications. Cardozo Law Rev 36: 1837–1915

Crootof R, Renz F (2017) An opportunity to change the conversation on autonomous weapon systems. Lawfare. https://www.lawfareblog.com/opportunity-change-conversation-autonomous-weapon-systems. Accessed 20 Dec 2022

de Mesquita BB, Smith A (2011) The dictator's handbook: why bad behavior is almost always good politics. PublicAffairs, New York

de Wolf AH (2006) Modern condottieri in Iraq: privatizing war from the perspective of international human rights law. Indiana J Glob Leg Stud 13:315–356

DeWinter-Schmitt R (2016) Transnational business governance through standards and codes of conduct. In: Abrahamsen R, Leander A (eds) Routledge handbook of private security studies. Routledge, London, pp 258–267

Elsea JK (2010) Private security contractors in Iraq and Afghanistan: legal issues. Congressional Research Service, Washington D.C.

Gaston EL (2008) Mercenarism 2.0? The rise of the modern private security industry and its implications for international humanitarian law enforcement. Harv Int Law J 49:221–248

Hasian M (2011) The Simon Mann Trial, the demise of the 'Dogs of War,' and the discursive legitimation of 'Humanitarian' private security companies in Africa. J Int Intercult Commun 4: 272–289

Hasler E (1994) Der Zeitreisende: Die Visionen des Henry Dunant. Nagel & Kimche, Zürich

Henckaerts J-M, Doswald-Beck L (eds) (2005) Customary international humanitarian law: Volume I: Rules. Cambridge University Press, Cambridge

Hoover MJ (1977) The laws of war and the Angolan trial of mercenaries: death to the dogs of war. Case West Res J Int Law 9:323–406

ICRC (2008) How is the term "Armed Conflict" defined in international humanitarian law. Geneva

Jo H (2015) Compliant rebels: rebel groups and international law in world politics. Cambridge University Press, Cambridge

Kälin W, Künzli J (2010) The law of international human rights protection. Oxford University Press, Oxford

Lesh M (2016) Direct participation in hostilities. In: Liivoja R, McCormack T (eds) Routledge handbook of the law of armed conflict. Routledge, London, pp 181–194

Lewis MW, Crawford E (2013) Drones and distinction: how IHL encouraged the rise of drones. Georgetown Journal of International Law 44:1127–1166

Maaß R (1990) Der Söldner und seine kriegsvölkerrechtliche Rechtsstellung als Kombattant und Kriegsgefangener. Universitätsverlag Brockmeyer, Bochum

Mancini M, Ntoubandi FZ, Marauhn T (2011) Old concepts and new challenges: are private contractors the mercenaries of the twenty-first century? In: Francioni F, Ronzitti N (eds) War by contract: human rights, humanitarian law, and private contractors. Oxford University Press, Oxford, pp 321–340

Marra WC, McNeil SK (2013) Understanding 'The Loop': regulating the next generation of war machines. Harv J Law Public Policy 36. https://doi.org/10.2139/ssrn.2043131

McClelland J (2003) The review of weapons in accordance with Article 36 of Additional Protocol I. Int Rev Red Cross 85:397–415

McFate S (2014) The modern mercenary: private armies and what they mean for world order. Oxford University Press, Oxford

Melzer N (2008) Targeted killing in international law. Oxford University Press, Oxford

Melzer N (2009) Interpretive guidance on the notion of direct participation in hostilities under international humanitarian law. ICRC, Geneva

Melzer N (2016) International humanitarian law: a comprehensive introduction. ICRC, Geneva

Percy S (2007) Mercenaries: strong norm, weak law. Int Organ 61:367–397

Percy S (2012) Regulating the private security industry: a story of regulating the last war. Int Rev Red Cross 94:941–960

Pictet JS (1952) Commentary on the Geneva conventions of 12 August 1949: Geneva convention for the amelioration of the condition of the wounded and sick in armed forces in the field. ICRC, Geneva

Renz F (2017) The role of private military and security companies: corporate dogs of war or civilians operating in hostile environments? Swiss Rev Int Eur Law 27:305–332

Renz F (2020) State responsibility and new trends in the privatization of warfare. Edward Elgar, Northampton

Richemond-Barak D (2014) Can self-regulation work? Lessons from the private security and military industry. Mich J Int Law 35:773–826

Rondeaux C (2019) Decoding the Wagner Group: analyzing the role of private military security contractors in Russian proxy warfare. New America Foundation. https://www.newamerica.org/international-security/reports/decoding-wagner-group-analyzing-role-private-military-security-contractors-russian-proxy-warfare/executive-summary-key-findings. Accessed 20 Dec 2022

Rowling JK (2003) Harry Potter and the order of the phoenix. Bloomsbury, London

Rowling JK (2005) Harry Potter and the half-blood prince. Bloomsbury, London

Rowling JK (2007) Harry Potter and the deathly hallows. Bloomsbury, London

Rowling JK (2015) Azkaban. https://www.wizardingworld.com/writing-by-jk-rowling/azkaban. Accessed 10 Dec 2022

Rowling JK (2016) Seventeenth century and beyond. https://www.wizardingworld.com/writing-by-jk-rowling/seventeenth-century-and-beyond-en. Accessed 1 Feb 2022

Sandoz Y, Swinarski C, Zimmermann B (eds) (1987) Commentary on the additional protocols of 8 June 1977 to the Geneva conventions of 12 August 1949. ICRC, Geneva

Sassòli M (2013) International law and the use and conduct of private military and security companies in armed conflicts. In: Companies in conflict situations: building a research network on business, conflicts and human rights. Institut Catalá Internacional

Sassòli M, Olson LM (2008) The relationship between international humanitarian law and human rights law where it matters: admissible killing and internment of fighters in non-international armed conflicts. Int Rev Red Cross 90:599–627

Scharre P (2018) Army of none: autonomous weapons and the future of war. W. W. Norton & Company, New York

Schmitt MN (2005) Humanitarian law and direct participation in hostilities by private contractors or civilian employees. Chic J Int law 5:511–546

Schmitt MN (2010) Deconstructing direct participation in hostilities: the constitutive elements. N Y Univ J Int Law Polit 42:697–739

Shaw MN (2017) International law, 8th edn. Cambridge University Press, Cambridge

Singer PW (2004) War, profits, and the vacuum of law: privatized military firms and international law. Columbia J Transnatl Law 42:521–549

Singer PW (2007) Corporate warriors, the rise of the privatized military industry (updated edition). Cambridge University Press, Cambridge

Solis GD (2010) The law of armed conflict: international humanitarian law in war. Cambridge University Press, Cambridge

Spear J (2006) Market forces: the political economy of private military companies. Fafo, Oslo

Taulbee JL (1985) Myths, mercenaries and contemporary international law. Calif West Int Law J 15:339–363

Thomson JE (1994) Mercenaries, pirates and sovereigns: state-building and extraterritorial violence in early modern Europe. Princeton University Press, Princeton

Tiefer C (2009) No more Nisour Squares: legal control of private security contractors in Iraq and after. Oregon Law Rev 88:745–776

Turns D (2014) The law of armed conflict (international humanitarian law). In: Evans MD (ed) International law. Oxford University Press, Oxford, pp 814–847

von Devivere D (2008) Unmittelbare Teilnahme an Feindseligkeiten: Kniefall des humanitären Völkerrechts vor der Wirklichkeit? Kritische Justiz 41:24–47

Watkin K (2005) Humans in the cross-hairs: targeting, assassination and extra-legal killing in contemporary armed conflict. In: Wippman D, Evangelista M (eds) New wars, new laws? Applying the laws of war in 21st century conflicts. Transnational, Ardsley, pp 137–179

Whitten JH (2012) They're getting away with murder: how the international criminal court can prosecute US private security contractors for the Nisour Square tragedy and why it should. Wash Univ Glob Stud Law Rev 11:503–525

Wyttenbach J (2014) Export von privaten Sicherheits- und Militärdienstleistungen: Regulierung durch Sitzstaaten. In: Kunz PV et al (eds) Berner Gedanken zum Recht: Festgabe der Rechtswissenschaftlichen Fakultät der Universität Bern für den Schweizerischen Juristentag 2014, pp 427–454

International Human Rights Law

4

Abstract

Even when there is no active conflict, there are plenty of concerns about the treatment of witches and wizards. Just think about the lack of a fair trial (whether Sirius or Hagrid), torture (from dementors to Umbridge's term at Hogwarts) and the treatment of house-elves. We will take a look at how lawyers would assess this and what ways might exist for witches and wizards to complain about human rights abuses.

4.1 What Is Human Rights Law?

4.1.1 A Brief Introduction to Human Rights

What are human rights? Yes, we are trying to answer the big questions now. As to why we are talking about this, the preamble (fancy way of saying introductory remarks) of the Universal Declaration of Human Rights states that the "recognition of the inherent dignity and of the equal and inalienable rights of all members of the human family is the foundation of freedom, justice and peace in the world." All clear now? Let's try a different way of getting closer to understanding what most of us recognize as human rights, how it translates into human rights law and what it means for us.

First of all: why do we think that humans have something called human rights? This builds on what most of us have agreed as basic entitlements of every human person. The ideal that there are inherent freedoms and intrinsic rights of every individual is part of the Euro-American tradition and dates back to the years of the Enlightenment.[1] This does not mean that no one before had discussed human rights. Indeed, there are many other references to human rights in the past before this. But

---

[1] Kälin and Künzli (2010), pp. 4–5.

the codification of human rights declarations of modern times is largely seen as dating back to the Virginia Declaration of Rights of 1776.[2] Don't let this fool you— it's not as if anyone had this figured out by 1776. When they were bravely claiming that all men were free and independent and had inherent rights, they were not referring to all men in the sense of really everyone you could think of. They were excluding women, enslaved people, just to name a few.[3] Yet, the overall intent of these treaties was that all human beings should have human rights (if we look at the preamble, rather than then treaties' implementation in practice). So in essence: yes, the majority of people believes that there are certain rights every person should have just because they are a human being. As you have been on this journey for a bit now, you will know that this is not as easy as it seems. There are relativist theories that take a different view, some based on a historical critique, others based on a cultural critique. And the debates in the Human Rights Council (HRC) frequently show that we are not as aligned in our thinking as one might hope. But we will leave this politically driven debate aside for now and will roll with the majority opinion that there are inherent human rights and that at least basic rights are relevant to all people across all cultures, political systems or beliefs.[4]

If we accept that there are certain rights that we just have by virtue of being human, the next obvious question is which rights and who gets to decide? More complicated. We won't go into the depth of all the different treaties that were developed over time but will stick to what is currently in place. The rest makes for a fascinating read and is highly recommended for further digging in your Hermione moments, but we'll keep it simple for the time being.[5]

When lawyers think about human rights law, they start out with the before mentioned Universal Declaration of Human Rights. Why is that? Well, after the end of the Second World War when the UN was founded, it included a reference to human rights in Art. 1 of its Charter, highlighting that one of its purposes was:

Art. 1 (3) UN Charter

To achieve international cooperation in solving international problems of an economic, social, cultural, or humanitarian character, and in promoting and encouraging respect for human rights and for fundamental freedoms for all without distinction as to race, sex, language, or religion.

With this general statement, the discussions began on what should be understood as human rights law. The UN Declaration of Human Rights is seen as the "common

---

[2]ibid.

[3]ibid.

[4]For one such example on this discussion: Shaw (2017), pp. 212 ff.

[5]More on the history of human rights law: Kälin and Künzli (2010), pp. 6 ff; Shaw (2017), pp. 213 ff.

standard of achievement for all peoples and nations",[6] meaning it is a legally non-binding document that summarizes the core points that all states were able to agree on when it was adopted by the UN General Assembly in 1948. Rights covered range from liberty and security of the person to equality before the law, due process, prohibition of torture, freedom of movement, asylum, the right to work and equal pay, the right to education and many more.

The good natured Hufflepuffs among you will now go "great that everyone was able to agree on the core rights, issue solved – let's move on and please explain what these rights are." I'm sure some of the Ravenclaws and Slytherins among the readers will likely raise their eyebrows. They are correct. The important point mentioned before was that this is solely a non-binding document. As we learned in the earlier chapters, non-binding means that while you express the intentions of upholding these obligations, you don't have to. There is therefore also no enforcement mechanism to ensure these obligations are upheld. So what did the lawyers and politicians do to ensure that we have more than nice words to back us up in our belief that there should be human rights for everyone? Let's have a look at the core treaties. But before we do that, let's understand the different categorizations of human rights.

4.1.2 Three Generations of Human Rights

To make matters even more complicated, lawyers have started distinguishing three generations of human rights. These generations are a reference, yes, you guessed correctly, to the time in which they became relevant.

First generation rights are the rights that concern your civil and political rights. Meaning whether your state guarantees your right to life, your liberty and allows you freedom of speech and freedom to exercise political rights (e.g., vote) while guaranteeing a fair trial. These just as examples—the list before is not exhaustive. They date back to the late eighteenth century and to the American as well as French declarations of human rights.[7] These are the rights that we will also look at in more detail when assessing the rights in the wizarding world. Just think about the right to life in the context of the killing curse and the right to a fair trial that should have been evoked by Sirius Black when he was shipped off to Azkaban.

Second generation rights are economic, social and cultural rights and date back to the nineteenth century (given the many issues that populations faced in the wake of industrialization). Relevant rights are the rights to food, shelter and health and the right to education.[8]

Third generation rights are solidarity or group rights such as the right to development, to peace and to a healthy environment. They are just now beginning to be

---

[6]Preamble, Universal Declaration of Human Rights.

[7]Kälin and Künzli (2010), p. 32.

[8]ibid.

incorporated into international law, such as in the African Charter on Human and Peoples' Rights (ACHPR).[9]

Depending on the country, there are very different views on how important the generations of human rights are. For example, for many developing countries the second generation rights are seen as more important compared to the first generation rights. A lot of this ties back to what is most relevant for the country in question, what culture they have, what their religion is etc. (playing back to the earlier point on a relativistic rather than universal theory of human rights).[10]

4.1.3   The Core Treaties to Remember

On an international level, there are nine core human rights instruments. Yes, I know, instrument is a strange term. Think of it as treaties that also have a committee of experts that monitors the implementation. In addition to the treaties, there are optional protocols. Meaning that if states had additional ideas later on or knew that certain ideas would not gather support of the majority, they placed them in an optional protocol.

The nine core human rights instruments are:

- International Convention on the Elimination of All Forms of Racial Discrimination (ICERD)
- International Covenant on Civil and Political Rights (ICCPR)
- International Covenant on Economic, Social and Cultural Rights (ICESCR)
- Convention on the Elimination of All Forms of Discrimination against Women (CEDAW)
- Convention against Torture and Other Cruel, Inhuman or Degrading Treatment or Punishment (CAT)
- Convention on the Rights of the Child (CRC)
- International Convention on the Protection of the Rights of All Migrant Workers and Members of Their Families (ICMW)
- International Convention for the Protection of All Persons from Enforced Disappearance (CPED)
- Convention on the Rights of Persons with Disabilities (CRPD)

Now please repeat. Just kidding. Yes, this is quite a range. And as mentioned, you'll have to also take a look at the optional protocols and understand which states have ratified these treaties to fully understand who has committed to what.[11]

---

[9]ibid.

[10]More on this in Shaw (2017), pp. 212 ff.

[11]For a link to the texts of these treaties, information on when they entered into force as well as further information on the topic of core human rights instruments, please refer to this website: OHCHR (2022b).

As you by now surely appreciate and love the complexities of law, beware that the international human rights treaties are not the only relevant ones. Add to that a full list of regional human rights treaties such as the ACHPR, the American Convention on Human Rights (ACHR) or the European Convention on Human Rights (ECHR), to just name a few.

Across these different treaties, several rights keep on repeating themselves. You might wonder why states bother to sign different treaties with overlapping content and what that means for how they have to uphold what they sign. Can they choose whichever version they feel like at any given point in time? Well, not really. The rule is quite simple. If your state signs three human rights treaties that all guarantee freedom of speech but to differing degrees, your state needs to continuously uphold the highest standard to which it signed up.

4.1.4 Positive and Negative Obligations

For every human right there are negative and positive obligations. Negative obligations means that there is a duty to respect. Positive obligations means there is a duty to protect and fulfill.[12] I know this does not give you a lot more clarity. Let's look at a practical example of what this means.

Taking the right to life and the negative obligation is simple—it means that your government should not kill you. But what does it mean for the positive obligations? Well, the government has the obligation to protect your right to life, for example by setting up a police system that hunts down murderers and makes sure they can't endanger the lives of others. Let's take the case of the killings by the death eaters during Voldemort's second rise to power. In that case the killings were certainly not committed by the government (clueless as they were) and they tried as good as they could to resolve them. This means they fulfilled their positive obligations.

The duty to fulfill as part of the positive obligations is a bit more tricky to understand and the right to life not the best example. Let's take the right to a fair trial for this one—the government has to set up a court system and relevant regulation that ensures this fair trial.[13] If it does this, then it has fulfilled the positive obligation under the right to a fair trial.

The obvious question with regard to these positive and negative obligations is: when are the positive obligations fulfilled? Think about it for a moment. The negative obligations are easy to fulfill—you just don't do the thing you're not allowed to do. Don't kill, don't take away people's freedom of expression, don't take away their freedom of movement. But how do you uphold positive obligations without going full on 1984 on people? If you don't understand this reference, you'll

---

[12]For more details on this distinction between positive and negative obligations: Renz (2020), pp. 82 ff.; de Wolf (2012), pp. 132–133.

[13]Yes, this is all oversimplified. For more on the distinctions, please go to the more sophisticated elaborations in Kälin and Künzli (2010), pp. 94 ff.

want to read this book as it will also open your eyes to many related issues going on today that sound astonishingly similar to the fiction in the book. Well, it is indeed not that easy. Take the right to life again—if you want to uphold the positive obligation to protect, does this mean you have to prevent anyone from being killed at all cost or just a majority of people? This is where a term lawyers love comes in: due diligence. You of course cannot prevent all instances of murder in your country at all times without infringing on a range of other rights of your people. So, due diligence. Basically, it means that if a state knew or must have known of a real and immediate risk it has to exercise the required standard of care to prevent a violation. Let's simplify this further. Imagine you are an official in Britain and you just got a call that innocent people were being killed. In this case, you certainly "knew" of the "real and immediate risk" to the life of other innocent people. Now what do they have to do? Mobilize the military and restrict all movement country-wide until the killer is found? Collect DNA samples for everyone residing within the country? Well, this would certainly meet the "standard of care" criterion but would not be reasonable to expect from the government in all such cases. Therefore, due diligence only requires that the government makes use of "all means reasonably available". Meaning you don't have to go full on mobilizing the military, it's fully sufficient if you launch a proper police investigation.[14] And yes, there have to be limits in how your reaction to one human rights violations impacts other human rights of your population (linking to the point of collecting DNA samples or mass surveillance—but we will leave this highly political topic for another discussion).

4.1.5 Who Has to Uphold Human Rights?

Now that we've covered the basics of human rights law, let's ask the core question: who has to uphold human rights? There is a limited number of options as to who could have the duty to uphold them: individuals, the international community and states. Let's go through these options for a moment and think about how this would work.

- Option 1: Individuals. Quite tricky—imagine you living in Little Whinging would be in charge of guaranteeing that the right to a fair trial is upheld if your neighbor Mrs. Figg decides to have her cats hunt down Dudley Dursley. There is no way that you would be able to guarantee a fair trial for her, even if you would be a superstar lawyer—no matter how much you complain, if the government does not set up the necessary courts and hires independent judges, there is little you as individual can do. For other rights you might have a role to play (e.g., not killing anyone), but you would also have limited ability to protect the lives of all people in Britain, unless you are Wonder Woman on a mission. So not likely that there is a distinct human rights obligation for individuals.

---

[14] More on the due diligence principle: Renz (2020), pp. 85 ff.; Kolb (2017), p. 63.

- Option 2: The international community. Now we're bringing in the big guns. The international community—well, there are always calls for support from the international community. Just take up the Muggle Daily Prophet equivalent in your country and you'll certainly find an article in which a struggling government fighting a rebel insurgency, the government of a developing country hit by natural disaster or a movement of self-declared freedom fighters calls on support from the international community. And there are instances in which this abstract body— the international community—has acted. Usually not in unison, all countries stepping in, but a large enough group of countries reacting to a perceived threat to international security, economic stability or a humanitarian crisis. Yet, when we think about particular human rights and how the international community could uphold both negative as well as positive obligations it becomes a bit more tricky. Imagine the right to a fair trial and the demand from the international community to uphold this. If you live in Philippines, how do you expect South Africa to fix this for you? Difficult to imagine. And except from extreme situations that trigger the responsibility to protect, the international community as such will have to be largely left out of these issues.[15]
- Option 3: States. Yes, you guessed correctly. States is the right answer. While individuals are the ones granted human rights, states are the ones who have to uphold them—both the negative as well as the positive obligations. States are also the ones who can get sued by individuals in case they do not uphold their obligations.[16] States are the ones that can guarantee the right to a fair trial by setting up the justice system in the necessary way. They can also step in if there is a rebel insurgency, if a natural disaster hits or if a serial killer is on the run.

4.1.6   The Big Question of Universality

Before we jump into the tricky questions of how to apply human rights to the wizarding world, there is one larger debate that needs to be at least mentioned here. The question of universality of human rights. What does universality mean in our context? Basically, it means that the same human rights should apply to people whether they live in the vicinity of Hogwarts School of Witchcraft and Wizardry, Beauxbatons Academy of Magic or Castelobruxo. At first sight, this might seem logical. Everyone should have the same fundamental rights, no matter where they live.[17]

---

[15] The responsibility to protect is a political (not legal) commitment to counter risks of genocide, war crimes, ethnic cleansing and crimes against humanity. More on this here: UN (2022) Responsibility to Protect. I'll let you read the news and be the judge as to whether the international community is doing a great job in upholding this commitment.

[16] More on states as duty-bearers: Kälin and Künzli (2010), pp. 77 f.

[17] More on this debate in: Kälin and Künzli (2010), pp. 3 ff., 18 ff.; Shaw (2017), pp. 212 ff. For the relativist discussion: Panikkar (1982).

This concept is often challenged by those promoting relativistic theories (relative = it depends on country/culture/circumstances). Why would anyone challenge universality of human rights? Well, the argument goes that the Universal Declaration either went too far regarding liberal traditions or not far enough. A big debate is between those placing emphasis on civil and political rights vs. those highlighting the importance of social and economic rights. The argument goes that while Western nations value civil and political rights above all else, Asian nations are culturally more inclined to value social and economic rights higher. In recent years, there were intense debates about whether the concept of universality is part of cultural hegemony.[18] This discussion is currently louder than it was for many years and for those of you interested in it, looking closer at debates and arguments in the UN HRC can provide a good overview of where we are at on an international political level.[19]

We will not attempt to resolve this debate here but beware, young lawyers, that this is a topic you'll have to dive into when you decide to become a human rights lawyer.[20]

4.2   Does Human Rights Law Apply to Witches and Wizards?

Now let's get into the real question you all had on your mind: do human rights apply to witches and wizards? We'll have to answer this question as there is unfortunately no satisfactory account of human rights in the wizarding world. So to make sure that Harry and his friends are sufficiently covered, we'll have to revert to human rights for now.

The question whether human rights law applies to witches and wizards again has two sub-components. First, we need to figure out whether witches and wizards in general are exempt from falling under human rights law. Second, we need to understand the implications of the fact that they are living in a wizarding state and therefore technically are not British citizens (except from Muggle-borns and Squibs, but more on that later).

4.2.1   Understanding Applicability of Human Rights in General

We now have to venture into the world of discussing applicability of human rights. More specifically, we need to understand the scope of application in personal terms, substantive terms, territorial terms and temporal terms.[21] Fancy way of saying for who, which rights, where and when. So let's take a closer look.

---

[18]More on this in Panikkar (1982) and Dundes Renteln (1990).

[19]Just giving you a starting point for this: Keaten (2022).

[20]To get you started on understanding the full extent of the debates: Kälin and Künzli (2010), pp. 18 ff.; Dundes Renteln (1990); Shaw (2017), pp. 210 ff.

[21]Kälin and Künzli (2010), p. 121.

Personal and territorial scope are the most tricky one in our context—we'll therefore look at this separately in the next chapters. Which rights and when is easier to solve for. And as a deeply pragmatic person I love to solve the quick wins first, so here we go.

Scope of protection means what exactly is protected under the human right. This basically means that for each human right we'll have to look into the relevant treaties and look at what it aims to protect. For example, for the right to education, you'll have to assess carefully whether it means that your government has to ensure that your basic education needs are covered or wants to fully fund you throughout your PhD and two post docs (hint—it might be the former).[22] And when you think you fully understood what the scope of protection is about, you'll also need to look into whether there are any reservations by the state that you are assessing. Reservations unfortunately don't have anything to do with you getting your favorite bar stool at the Hog's Head. Instead, it means that a state has said that while it in general agrees to what the treaty is about, it might not like all the statements in it and therefore wants to exclude let's say Articles 5 and 17. Now, not everything can be excluded and we won't go into the full details of how this works. But beware that there will be numerous cases in which there is an exception given such a reservation and we need to understand them before making any judgments about whether there were human rights violations.[23]

The second challenge that we can resolve as more of a quick win is that of **temporal application**—meaning "when" do human rights apply. You all know the scenario—5 years ago you were asked what your favorite drink is, you carelessly answered butterbeer and now you get butterbeer at every visit. Governments can feel the same way. Now what if you as a government agreed to a treaty but now no longer feel like upholding it as the situation has changed. Maybe just as a matter of political convenience, maybe because you are facing difficult circumstances such as a national emergency (typhoons, flooding, you name it) or conflict. In general, states have to uphold human rights law from the moment they ratified the treaty and it entered into force. Yet, they can either denunciate or derogate from their obligations. Denunciation means that you declare that you no longer intend to uphold the treaty. Derogation means that states can stop adhering to certain rights during times of emergency. Imagine for example the right to education—in case of war you could not ask the government to ensure that all kids are going to school. Not everyone has the nerve to run such a high-risk operation as Hogwarts.[24]

---

[22] More on the scope of protection in Kälin and Künzli (2010), p. 125.

[23] More on the scope of protection in Kälin and Künzli (2010), pp. 125 ff.; Shaw (2017), pp. 693 ff. For a detailed discussion see Zvobgo et al. (2020), pp. 785–797.

[24] Kälin and Künzli (2010), pp. 142–144.

4.2.2   Personal Scope for Witches and Wizards

The first question is: are witches and wizards considered human and therefore can have human rights? Let's make this simple—why shouldn't they be? They are living and breathing human beings, they only have add-on features (meaning their magical abilities). It's not as if people with super soccer skills are excluded from human rights, or people who are really good at singing (well, there might be a case to make, but that might also just be my personal jealousy speaking). At the same time, people with disability are obviously protected under human rights treaties and get special protection in some additional treaties. So yes, in short, however you interpret the ability to do magic, witches and wizards are human beings and as such fall under the group protected by the rights. Some of you might argue that this is not fully correct, given that there are slight differences in physiology between Muggles and wizards (as highlighted by Newt Scamander during his successful journey throughout New York City), but given that Muggle-born witches and wizards exist and that there are no inherent obvious differences in their, well, humanity, we will really just assume that these are add-on features, rather than completely different species.

So what else is there to consider? Well, some rights are for all humans and some only for citizens. This might actually make a difference, in particular to pure-blood witches and wizards. Most human rights are applicable to all humans regardless of where they are from (e.g., right to life). Political rights (e.g., right to vote) of course can't just be claimed by everyone visiting Little Whinging from a foreign country to admire the perfectly kept lawns. These rights are for citizens only. There are some other exceptions as well—take the Convention on the Elimination of All Forms of Discrimination against Women.[25] You guessed correctly—this is a right that might apply to Hermione but not to Ron. But overall, there is no reason to believe that witches and wizards would not be covered by the personal scope of at least those rights that apply to all humans.[26]

For the human rights only applying to citizens, the situation for Squibs is quite clear. As Mrs. Figg highlighted during her visit to the Wizengamot, the Ministry of Magic did not have a record of her. This means she must be fully covered by Muggle laws and therefore also a full-on citizen of Muggle Britain. We'll have to assume that there is a type of process in place to ensure that Squibs are covered in all relevant Muggle registries. For those of you wondering, Squibs are children born to wizarding families that do not have the ability to do magic.

For Muggle-born witches and wizards, as previously noted, we'll also assume that they retain dual-citizenship with their Muggle government.[27] It is more complicated for so-called pure-bloods. Yet, to be fair, the rights limited to citizens might also not be the most critical rights for witches and wizards. Or at least we'll have to

---

[25] More on this in Shaw (2017), pp. 244–246.

[26] Kälin and Künzli (2010), pp. 121–123.

[27] This was discussed in Sect. 2.1.2.

assume that they don't care deeply about Muggle politics and their ability to get involved in them (of course aside from protecting the Muggle Prime Minister).

4.2.3 Territorial Scope in the Wizarding World

Now on to our last question regarding applicability: territorial scope. This basically covers where exactly states have to uphold the human rights they commit to. The easiest scenario is of course if the violation of human rights occurs within the territory of the state we are talking about.[28] This is a clear case—territorial scope is given. But how about any violations outside of the territory of the state? Imagine a few different scenarios around extraterritorial application (yes, it basically means "if something happens in a different country"):

- Scenario 1: Ministry officials of state A (for simplicity sake, let's say Ministry officials on an official mission) violate human rights in state B.
- Scenario 2: Ministry officials of state A violate human rights in state B—but state A is occupying that territory.

The answer to these questions depends on the relevant treaty we are looking into. As I mentioned numerous times before in this book, lawyers thrive on complexity. So yes, there is no universal answer to the question of territorial application. For some treaties, territorial scope is linked to all persons under the jurisdiction of a state (e.g., ECHR). For other treaties, it is linked to territory and jurisdiction (e.g., ICCPR).[29] In yet other cases, it is linked to "any territory under its jurisdiction" (e.g., CAT). Considering all of this, how do we make sense across all the different treaties? We'll follow the lead of other legal scholars.

When we are outside of the national territory of state A, this state is only bound by a treaty if its state agents (imagine Percy on an official mission if he were working for the ministry) violate human rights.[30] This now leaves us with an answer for Scenario 1. In this case, the territorial scope is given as they were state officials on an official mission.

But what if we are dealing with Scenario 2 in which state B is occupied by state A? In these cases, the rules around jurisdiction will be useful again and we can assume that if state A has jurisdiction over the territory and is in control of it, it also

---

[28] Kälin and Künzli (2010), p. 132.

[29] There are lengthy debates about how to interpret the "and" in Art. 2 ICCPR and whether both territory and jurisdiction have to be given. If you are keen to look into this in more detail, please take this book off your library shelf: Kälin and Künzli (2010), pp. 133–134.

[30] Kälin and Künzli (2010), pp. 129–134.

has to uphold human rights commitments it made.[31] So even in Scenario 2, state A is bound by its obligations—and not by the obligations that state B had entered into.

4.2.4   Our Checklist for Human Rights Violations Towards Witches and Wizards

If you want to assess whether any human rights were violated, always think through the following:[32]

– Has a witch or wizard been harmed (if not, why are we talking about it)?
– Was the right in question protected (e.g., did the state we want to take to court have a reservation in place regarding this specific right)?
– Was the witch or wizard a protected person (e.g., does the right apply to all humans or only citizens, if only citizens, is our witch or wizard Muggle-born)?
– Is the witch or wizard currently within the jurisdiction of the Muggle state (e.g., is the witch at King's Cross station but not in Hogsmeade)?
– Was the right in question currently in force (e.g., if there would have been full on conflict with Voldemort affecting the Muggles more than it did, they might have derogated from certain rights)?
– Has the state you want to sue either violated its negative or positive obligations (e.g., did said state know of the presence of serial killers, but preferred to just sit this one out as the portrait of the other minister told the Muggle prime minister not to worry)?
– Is there a way for the government to justify the violation?

And to ensure that you keep on the watch for all types of violations while we get deeper in the human rights law, I heartily recommend that you look into the list of potential human rights violations committed against Tom Riddle. Yes, you read that correctly. Only because someone is evil does not mean that all their rights seize to exist.[33]

4.3   Can Wizards Raise Human Rights Complaints?

Now that we have started to understand the basics of human rights law, let's move into the really tricky issues. When there actually is a human rights violation—where do you go and complain about it? Remember the initial statement about our anarchic international society and the need for states to agree to being subject of a court's

---

[31] For more on the fascinating question of whether human rights law can be applied outside of the territory of a state, take a look here: da Costa (2013), pp. 9–14.

[32] For a more serious checklist, please refer to Kälin and Künzli (2010), p. 149.

[33] For more on this fascinating topic, please refer to: Watson (2010).

jurisdiction? This comes into play here. What we'll need to understand first is jurisdiction of human rights courts, meaning when and where can you actually go and complain at a court about a state violating your human rights. Now before you start visualizing Arthur Weasley at the European Court of Human Rights (ECtHR), let's get a basic understanding of how the court system works.

4.3.1   How Are Human Rights Enforced?

On the question on how human rights are enforced, some cynics might answer: poorly. The answer is, however, more differentiated than that. In fact, there are several ways in which human rights are enforced. Broadly, we need to differentiate between what states do to enforce human rights law at a national and an international level. Given that our book conveniently focuses on international law, we'll skip over the discussion of national enforcement of human rights. But to give the curious minds among you at least a sense of what this would be—imagine your government enacting legislation to protect human rights or launching human rights dialogues with other nations.[34]

Now back to the international level. Again, there are different levels to it. We have the human rights mechanisms that are either based on the UN Charter (e.g., HRC) or specific treaties (e.g., ECtHR) and the criminal tribunals such as the ICC. The ICC will be covered in our international criminal law section.[35] Here, we'll take a look at the HRC and ECtHR as two examples for human rights mechanisms on the international level.

4.3.1.1 Human Rights Council

The HRC is one of the charter-based UN bodies, meaning its basis is the 1945 Charter of the UN. The HRC was created by the UN General Assembly (GA) in 2006 and is the main UN organ dealing with human rights issues. It replaced the Commission on Human Rights that had been in place since 1946.[36] 47 nations are elected as members of the HRC and they are tasked with protecting and promoting human rights.[37] Now, clever folks among you will think, how should it do this? Remember the entire problem around state sovereignty. So how does the HRC deal with this?

There are four tools the HRC uses to fulfill its tasks: (1) Universal Periodic Review (UPR), (2) a system of special procedures, (3) a system of expert advice and (4) complaint procedure. I agree, this does not necessarily sound as convincing as

---

[34] Kälin and Künzli (2010), p. 184.

[35] See Sect. 5.6.

[36] If you are dying to learn more about why it was replaced, refer to the following book: Kälin and Künzli (2010), pp. 240 ff.

[37] For a complete list of its tasks please refer to: General Assembly Resolution 60/251, available at: https://www2.ohchr.org/english/bodies/hrcouncil/docs/A.RES.60.251_En.pdf.

threatening human rights offenders with a visit by the dementors (well, when they were still part of the security apparatus). But let's hold off the disappointed grimace for a moment. Among these, let's assess what we would leverage in case our human rights are violated. We'll approach this from a more pragmatic angle. While all of these tools have their merit, let's be honest, not all will make equal sense to you as an individual in case of specific human rights violations.

The UPR certainly serves the purpose of raising bigger issues and making sure the international community is aware of them—yet, as an individual, this is not the right way to go.[38] Special procedures refer to independent experts who work either as part of working groups or Special Rapporteurs.[39] Their mandate is to examine and monitor specific human rights situations. Depending on the human rights issue you are facing, this might help in ensuring that the topic is surfaced (just think about the possibility to launch a working group on human rights violations of squibs).[40] Still, if you want to complain about one specific issue you have in mind, not the way to go.

The HRC Advisory Committee—as the name indicates—prepares studies and gives advice. Yet, it won't solve your specific human rights challenge. This leaves, you guessed correctly, the complaint procedure. Yes, this sounds exactly what you would look for if you aim to complain about the lack of a fair trial in case a house-elf dropped a dessert and you were blamed. But is it really? Let's look into it. Under the complaint procedure, individuals, groups and non-governmental organizations (NGOs) can submit communications if they claim to be victims of human rights violations or know of such violations.[41] Once the communication (meaning your complaint) is submitted, it has to go through four stages.[42] First, the Chairperson of the Working Group on Communications (yes, of course there is another working group) has to screen your communication (this is basically sense checking what has been written and seeing whether you are allowed to submit this communication). The second stage is a check by the Working Group on Communication that looks in more detail through your complaint and assesses whether it has merit (meaning might be true) and if it should be dismissed, kept under review (asking the state about which you complained to provide further information) or whether it should be moved on to (yes, yet another working group) the Working Group on Situations. Your communication now becomes a situation. The Working Group on Situations meets two times per year and has to decide whether to stop looking into the situation you complained about, whether they want to review it further or send it off to the

---

[38] Kälin and Künzli (2010), pp. 244 ff.

[39] Special Rapporteurs means that are appointed by the HRC. They are independent experts who report or advise on human rights related issues either linked to a specific topic (e.g., human rights and transnational corporations) or to a specific country (e.g., Afghanistan). More on the current mandate holders here: https://www.ohchr.org/en/special-procedures-human-rights-council/current-and-former-mandate-holders-existing-mandates.

[40] Kälin and Künzli (2010), pp. 244 ff.

[41] More on the options for individual complaints procedures: Kälin and Künzli (2010), pp. 219 ff.

[42] For a good explanation of these four steps, take a look at OHCHR (2022c).

HRC. The last one only happens when they believe that what you complained about shows "consistent patterns of gross and reliably attested violations of human rights and fundamental freedoms".[43] Final stage—you guessed correctly—is the HRC. The HRC has to examine the report submitted by the Working Group on Situations. The options it has are:

- "discontinue considering the situation when further consideration or action is not warranted;
- keep the situation under review and request the State concerned to provide further information within a reasonable period of time;
- keep the situation under review and appoint an independent and highly qualified expert to monitor the situation and report back to the Council;
- discontinue reviewing the matter under the confidential complaint procedure in order to take up public consideration of the same;
- recommend to OHCHR to provide technical cooperation, capacity building assistance or advisory services to the State concerned."[44]

You might wonder—what does this mean—this does not seem as if the HRC can actually tell a state to stop doing what it is doing. You are correct. A state run by the sister of Dolores Umbridge could go wild and all the HRC would be able to do about it is review, appoint Special Rapporteurs or provide capacity building to the state concerned. Cynics among you will laugh out loud and say "great, let's help those states by building capacity". This idea is not as bad as it sounds—but yes, I understand the sentiment that there needs to be more. So let's circle back to the most important notion in public international law: sovereignty of states. If we accept sovereignty, we cannot ask for states to be held accountable by an international committee without the state explicitly signing up for it. Unless the crimes committed outweigh the need to protect state sovereignty and immunity. We'll look into that in our chapter on international criminal law.[45] But until then, the core take-away is that if you are looking for a way to complain about human rights violations and hope to see something done about it (such as a judgment issued), the HRC will not be your way forward. But there are other ways. They are always linked to specific treaties, as those were signed by the states and contain clauses that highlight that there will be enforcement mechanisms.

The enforcement mechanisms and their rules vary treaty by treaty. We'll take the example of the ECtHR because Harry lives in Europe.

---

[43] OHCHR (2022a).

[44] OHCHR (2022a).

[45] If you can't wait, jump ahead to Chap. 5.

4.3.1.2 ECtHR

The ECtHR is a court that belongs to the Council of Europe (CoE) and interprets the ECHR.[46] This is not to be confused with any European Union (EU) agency. You'll recognize that instantly when looking at the list of its members. Even if you have been paying the same level of attention in your politics class as Ron and Harry did in History of Magic, you should be able to figure out that this is more than the EU has. Moreover, many of the members are clearly not on the list of countries you would confuse as EU member states, such as Switzerland and Britain.[47] And this is where Harry comes into play again, given his ties to Britain. Even though Brexit cost Harry the chance of an EU passport, the ECtHR still remains relevant. Well, for now at least. If you are sure that Britain has left the CoE, please check the date of publication of this book—it might explain where the discrepancy results from.[48]

The ECtHR is in charge when it comes to alleged violations of the ECHR by any of the states that signed the treaty (remember, all those CoE member states). Any individual, NGO, group of individuals or contracting state (any of them) can complain about a human rights violation. This means there are two types of procedures—one linked to individuals complaining, the other one being intrastate cases (meaning one state complains about the other one).

Given the Statute of Secrecy it is not highly likely that any wizarding state will launch an intrastate complaint with the ECtHR (as that state would first have to join the CoE and ratify the ECHR, it might counteract the entire secrecy idea). So let's focus on the individual complaint and let me walk you through that process. I promise, there are less working groups than with the HRC.

Let's imagine Hermione's cousin has been the victim of a human rights violation. Law abiding as she is, Hermione does not take matters into her own hands (or rather wand) and advises her to complain with the ECtHR about the violation. First, she'll have to go through the legal proceedings in the UK. Why? Well, simply because we first want to give the relevant state the chance to right any wrong that was committed. Also, the relevant state (Britain in our case) will have an easier time assessing the merit of the case (meaning whether a violation actually happened). With the entire discussion about state sovereignty, it is also generally preferred to give states first a chance to resolve on their own, rather than directly rushing off to a high-flying international court and make your own government look bad (as well as contribute to the heavy caseload and limited resources of such courts).[49]

Say Hermione's cousin has done all of that but the court did not rule as she had hoped. Now she can send her complaint to the ECtHR (called an "application", don't

---

[46] More on the ECHR and ECtHR in Shaw (2017), pp. 255 ff.; Kälin and Künzli (2010), pp. 226 ff.

[47] For a full list of members refer to CoE (2022) 46 Member States.

[48] Since starting on this writing journey, the number already had to be modified from 47 to 46 given that Russia left the CoE.

[49] Art. 35 I ECHR clearly states that first all "domestic remedies" have to be exhausted—meaning you try to complain to all the courts you can complain to in your own country, taking it up to the highest level. After this, you get to complain to the ECtHR.

ask me why). First, the court checks whether her application is admissible. This means a check of four criteria:

1) exhaustion of domestic remedies (did you try to win your court case in the relevant country already and failed),
2) 4-month deadline to file your application (you only have 4 months from the final judicial decision, so better hurry up),
3) the complaint has to be based on the ECHR (makes sense, you can't complain about a violation against the Ban on Experimental Breeding in front of those Muggle judges) and
4) the applicant needs to have suffered a significant disadvantage.[50]

Let's assume all four of those are given (this being Hermione's cousin we can assume that she was well-prepared and did not miss any deadlines). Now, the Court has to make a judgment on whether or not there was a violation of the ECHR. I'll spare you the details of this as this would require going right by right. We'll look into some rights in the following, so don't be disappointed just yet. But let's just assume that Hermione's cousin was right to complain and that her human rights were severely violated. Now what? Yes, you guessed it—there are several options. The way in which the judgment of the court is implemented depends on the state. But they are not unsupervised. Instead, the Council of Ministers of the CoE (basically what the inquisitorial squad was to Hogwarts in Harry's 5th year) monitors whether states pay damages and implement the judgment (e.g., change legislation if that was the problem to begin with). Yes, I hear you. This is a bit as if you place the Weasley twins in charge of enforcing Hogwarts rules. In the beginning, this system actually worked surprisingly well—in recent years there were, however, several cases in which judgments were disregarded or just not completely implemented.[51] Yet, compared to the option of having the UN think about your complaint for a year and then maybe send special rapporteurs to your country, let's take this as a "win" for justice. Also, as always in international relations, there is the added benefit of the court case you launch leading to publicity.[52] And there is hardly a more effective court than the court of public opinion.

---

[50] More on this in ECHR (2022). For a more detailed overview of how this process works: Kälin and Künzli (2010), pp. 227ff.

[51] ibid., pp. 230 ff.

[52] Just a few examples of "famous" cases that were heard before the ECtHR and caused publicity: Murphy (2022) and Bowcott (2014).

4.3.2   What Options Would Witches and Wizards Have to Launch a Complaint?

Let's assume that witches and wizards have experienced human rights violations and want to launch complaints about these. What options do they have? Well, there are again different scenarios. The core question is whether the human rights violation was conducted in a wizarding or a Muggle state.

If it was conducted in a wizarding state, we have to hope that the wizarding community was smart enough to set up their own human rights mechanism, meaning a Wizarding Court of Human Rights (WCHR) and we have just not heard about it so far. Otherwise, we only have the options under international criminal law left—for worst cases of offenses.

If the human rights violation was conducted in a state, we have to check which human rights treaties the state has ratified. In those treaties, we then have to test for personal scope to assess if the right only applies to nationals (would be difficult for witches and wizards, unless they are Muggle-born and have dual citizenship). Beyond these treaties, we could also look into the mechanisms based on the UN Charter as they apply to all nations. As any individual can submit a complaint to the HRC there would be no difficulty for witches and wizards to do so. But yes, I agree with your thinking—a treaty-based complaint procedure seems more appealing. Whether or not this is possible, well, you'll get the lawyer response here: it depends. So you'll have to help your witch and wizard friends in figuring this out, case by case.[53]

4.4   A Look into One Specific Right: The Right to a Fair Trial

After having looked into the basics of human rights law, it is about time that we get more specific. One human rights concern that got repeatedly triggered when learning more about the wizarding world is the right to a fair trial. The number of cases are manifold and we'll take a closer look at them down the line—just think about Dobby using magic and Harry getting into trouble, Hagrid's stint at Azkaban when he was suspected of opening the chamber of secrets or Sirius' time in Azkaban for the alleged killing of those Muggles and Peter Pettigrew.

4.4.1   What Does a Fair Trial Look Like?

Before assessing the many ways in which the wizarding world obviously seems to disregard a right to a fair trial, let's get a sense of what it should look like if they were

---

[53] The analogy to this stateless people. For more on how their rights are protected, given that they cannot rely on protection as a country's national, check out: https://www.unhcr.org/un-conventions-on-statelessness.html.

to follow our law on this. As we had discussed earlier, human rights are often detailed out in numerous treaties. The right to a fair trial is an excellent example to highlight how many treaties there are with similar or the same content. Human rights related to principles in criminal proceedings can be found in Art. 14 and 15 ICCPR, Art. 8 and 9 ACHR,[54] Art. 15–17 and Art. 19 Arab Charter on Human Rights (ArCHR),[55] Art. 7 ACHPR,[56] Art. 6 and 7 ECHR and Art. 40 CRC—among others. Now we'll take an in-depth look into each of these rights and will compare the nuances. Just kidding.[57] We'll make our life easy and will just look at Art. 14 ICCPR to get a basic understanding of what we mean when they talk about a fair trial. Beware, Art. 14 ICCPR is one of the long ones. On the bright side, I'll walk you through it step by step. Yet, I'll want you to go ahead and at least skim through it on your own. To make your life a little easier, I have taken the liberty to add highlights (yes, the legal text as such is not boldened to make your reading experience more pleasant).

The following will only be limited to the core rights. As always, there is more to it. But that will be left for your own light reading experience.[58]

Art. 14 ICCPR

1. All persons shall be **equal before the courts and tribunals**. In the determination of any criminal charge against him, or of his rights and obligations in a suit at law, everyone shall be entitled to a **fair and public hearing by a competent, independent and impartial tribunal established by law**. The press and the public may be excluded from all or part of a trial for reasons of morals, public order (ordre public) or national security in a democratic society, or when the interest of the private lives of the parties so requires, or to the extent strictly necessary in the opinion of the court in special circumstances where publicity would prejudice the interests of justice; but any judgement rendered in a criminal case or in a suit at law shall be made public except where the interest of juvenile persons otherwise requires or the proceedings concern matrimonial disputes or the guardianship of children.
2. Everyone charged with a criminal offence shall have the right to be **presumed innocent until proved guilty** according to law.
3. In the determination of any criminal charge against him, everyone shall be entitled to the following **minimum guarantees**, in full equality:

---

[54] (Inter-) American Convention on Human Rights of 22 November 1969; 1144 UNTS 123, OAS TS No 36.

[55] Arab Charter on Human Rights of 22 May 2004; reprinted in 12 International Human Rights Reports 893 (2005)

[56] African Charter on Human and Peoples' Rights (Banjul Charter) of 27 June 1981; 1520 UNTS 217, OAU Doc CAB/LEG/67/3 rev. 5.

[57] If you are severely disappointed right now, please look here: Kälin and Künzli (2010), pp. 440 ff.

[58] Kälin and Künzli (2010), pp. 440 ff.; Weissbrodt (2014).

    a. To be **informed promptly** and in detail in a language which he understands of the **nature and cause of the charge** against him;

    b. To have **adequate time and facilities for the preparation of his defence** and to **communicate with counsel of his own choosing;**

    c. To be **tried without undue delay;**

    d. To be tried in his presence, and to **defend himself in person** or through **legal assistance** of his own choosing; to be informed, if he does not have legal assistance, of this right; and to have legal assistance assigned to him, in any case where the interests of justice so require, and without payment by him in any such case if he does not have sufficient means to pay for it;

    e. To **examine,** or have examined, the **witnesses against him** and to **obtain the attendance** and **examination of witnesses on his behalf** under the same conditions as witnesses against him;

    f. To have the **free assistance of an interpreter** if he cannot understand or speak the language used in court;

    g. **Not to be compelled to testify against himself** or to confess guilt.

4. In the case of **juvenile persons**, the procedure shall be such as will **take account of their age** and the desirability of promoting their rehabilitation.

5. Everyone convicted of a crime shall have the right to his **conviction and sentence being reviewed by a higher tribunal** according to law.

6. When a person has by a final decision been convicted of a criminal offence and when subsequently his **conviction has been reversed** or he has been **pardoned** on the ground that a new or newly discovered fact shows conclusively that there has been a miscarriage of justice, the person who has suffered punishment as a result of such conviction shall be **compensated** according to law, unless it is proved that the non-disclosure of the unknown fact in time is wholly or partly attributable to him.

7. No one shall be liable to be tried or **punished again for an offence for which he has already been finally convicted or acquitted** in accordance with the law and penal procedure of each country.

4.4.1.1 Right to Equality Before Courts and a Fair and Public Hearing

Details on the right to equality before courts and a fair and public hearing can be found in Art. 14 (1) ICCPR—that and in many other treaties of course.[59] There are three components to this right. First, equality before the courts. Second, a fair and public hearing. Third, the right to be tried by a competent, independent and impartial tribunal established by the law. Let's take this one by one.

Equality before the courts means "that the same procedural rights are to be provided to all parties. . .".[60] Yes, there is more to the statement. But this is what I'll need you to remember. The same rights have to be granted to all those involved in a

---

[59] You can find more on this in Kälin and Künzli (2010), p. 449.

[60] HRC, General Comment No 32 (2007), para 13. See more on this in Kälin and Künzli (2010), p. 451.

court case. This means that both prosecutor and defendant (the person being accused) have to be allowed to appeal a decision (saying you disagree and want a higher ranking court to take a look at the decision) and the court has to take all evidence into account (yes, you'll immediately think about Mrs. Figg's testimony regarding the dementors that was almost not heard).

The goal of having a **fair and public hearing** is not to embarrass the defendant in front of the public. The goal is to ensure that the judges are independent and impartial and there should not be any hostility from the public in the court room or any type of influence or intimidation towards the judges. Public hearings ensure that the judges face public scrutiny for how the trial is run. They are, however, not necessary. In some cases the media and public can be excluded (linked to concerns about national security or to protect witnesses[61]). In other cases—such as when during an appeal the court is arguing about the exact interpretation of the law—there will not be public hearings.[62]

The last aspect sounds like fun—a **competent, independent and impartial tribunal**. Yes, roll your eyes. This seems like a no-brainer. But it unfortunately tends to be one of the more tricky aspects. A criminal proceeding has to be led by a tribunal. It can't just be any administrative body that is handing out sentences. So far so good. Independence links to everything from procedure to the appointment of judges as well as whether anyone tries to interfere with the judgment in the specific case. Impartiality refers to two aspects. First, the judges cannot have any preconceptions regarding the case. Second, the tribunal as such must appear impartial to a reasonable observer.[63] This essentially means that if you as an unbiased, objective person take a look at what is going on it should not smell fishy.

Thinking about all those aspects, I'm sure you'll have plenty of examples in mind where the wizarding world is clearly falling short off the requirements. We'll take a look at these in a bit.

4.4.1.2 Presumption of Innocence

The presumption of innocence is listed in Art. 14 (2) ICCPR (and yes, as with all of these, also in many, many other treaties[64]). This is an easy one—you have to first figure out if a person is guilty before saying so. Seems not too complicated. Simple examples are that senior administration officials should not publicly state that a person is guilty until the trial is done.[65] It also means that it is not the accused who has to prove his or her innocence. Instead, the prosecutor has to prove the guilt of the

---

[61] More on the right to a public hearing in criminal proceedings: Trechsel (2005) and Weissbrodt (2014). National security concerns in this context mean that if it is likely that information shared during the hearing could be a risk to national security, there is an incentive to prevent the public from becoming aware of this.

[62] More in this in Kälin and Künzli (2010), p. 453.

[63] More in this in Kälin and Künzli (2010), pp. 451 f.

[64] More in Art. 8 (2) ACHR; Art. 7 (1) ACHPR; Art. 16 ArCHR; Art. 6 (2) ECHR. Also take a look at Kälin and Künzli (2010), p. 454.

[65] More in this in Kälin and Künzli (2010), pp. 453 f.

accused. To give you an easy example—the government can't just tell the public that you stole Omnioculars and ship you off to prison because you can't prove that you didn't. Instead, the governments needs to prove that you stole those Omnioculars. And yes, I know what you are thinking—this does not seem to be what is done in the wizarding world.

4.4.1.3 Rights During the Trial

Rights during the trial are listed down in Art. 14 (3) ICCPR and are not just as easy to follow as the previous right. These are minimum guarantees, so yes, governments are free to do better than this. They should not do less. Really not. These minimum rights are (and you'll get this in plain English as no need to overcomplicate here):

- Tell people what they are accused of in a way and language they understand
- Give the person accused enough time to prepare their defense and talk to their lawyer (whom they chose)
- Don't delay the trial
- Make sure that the accused is present during the trial and is able to either defend themselves or be defended by a lawyer (whom they have to be able to choose freely—and in case they can't afford, get financial support for)
- Allow the accused to bring their own witnesses (for their innocence) and examine witnesses that accuse them
- Get support from an interpreter in case there are language issues
- Not to testify against oneself or be asked to confess guilt[66]

I won't give you examples of this here, mainly, as the wizarding world offers so many of them and we'll get around to them in a bit. So just hang in there (it is literally the next section).

4.4.2 Sirius and His 12 Years in Azkaban

Let's now get to our first case study of serious issues related to the fair trial. We'll have a field day with this. Our case concerns Sirius Black who spent 12 years in Azkaban for allegedly killing 12 Muggles and Peter Pettigrew.[67] In our world, this would make for quite the spectacular murder case. It might even warrant a John Grisham novel linked to the topic.

Yet, when looking at this case, no mentioning of a trial comes to mind. Instead, the Head of the Magical Law Enforcement Squad, Bartemius Crouch Sr., sent Black to Azkaban for 12 years until he famously escaped. Yes, there were plenty of eye witnesses, but as Sirius told Harry, they did not see what they thought they had seen.

---

[66]More in this in Kälin and Künzli (2010), pp. 453 f.

[67]More on this case in: Rapp (2010), pp. 91–101. Sharing the stories about Sirius Black's alleged crimes: Rowling (1999), Chapter 10: The Marauder's Map.

Reflecting on what we just learned about the rights to a fair trial, we will assess which of these rights were violated in Sirius' case. The first aspect that comes to mind is the right to equality before courts and a fair and public hearing (e.g., Art. 14 (1) ICCPR). We don't even have to dig into whether the court was independent or impartial—there was no hearing at all. This can be seen as a clear violation. Moreover, there was clearly no assumption of innocence until the trial is done as we just established that there was no trial. So we also have a violation of Art. 14 (2) ICCPR.

We don't have to go further than this as there are no rights that could have been violated during the trial as we never got that far. Now what could Sirius have done about this? Unfortunately, very little. For the crime he was accused of, there seems to be an agreement between the wizarding world and the Muggle world that jurisdiction lies with the wizarding world.[68] Therefore, it was fully up to the wizarding world to put Sirius on trial. Yes, I know, they didn't. But there is also no evidence that the wizarding world ratified any of the relevant treaties such as the ICCPR. There is therefore also no way for Sirius to launch a formal legal complaint—aside from the obvious challenge that such a complaint would have resulted in revealing a lot of secrets about the wizarding world and thereby violating the Statute of Secrecy. While the approach to bring Sirius behind bars in Azkaban is appalling, there did not seem to be a contradictory rule in wizarding law.

4.4.3   Hagrid and the Chamber of Secrets Allegations

Another case for clear miscarriage of justice and wrongful conviction is Hagrid. And it did not only hit him once, poor guy. The first time—you'll remember this for sure—was when Hagrid was still a student at Hogwarts and framed by Tom Riddle. The people in charge—whoever they were—seemed convinced that he was guilty and let his pet Acromantula roam free (after allegedly opening the chamber of secrets), eventually killing Myrtle Warren (the girl that then turned into Moaning Myrtle, yes, the toilet ghost). As punishment, they snapped his wand and expelled him. Given Dumbledore's insistence, he was allowed to stay at Hogwarts and was trained as gamekeeper.[69]

Again, we don't know of any actual trial that took place and therefore see similar violations of the right to a fair trial as in Sirius's case (in particular Art. 14 (1) and 14 (2) ICCPR).

But then all of this happened again for a second time. The Chamber of Secrets was opened, Hagrid was accused and then sent to Azkaban. Again, no trial. Minister of Magic Fudge just dropped by his place and arrested him.[70] This also shows that there is clearly no separation of power as we are used to in many Muggle nations

---

[68] See the discussion on this in Sect. 2.3.

[69] More on this in: Rowling (1998), Chapter 13: The Very Secret Diary

[70] Rowling (1998), Chapter 14: Cornelius Fudge.

(with an executive, legislative and judicative branch of government). Once again, clear violations of the right to a fair trial. There is also no sign that once he was exonerated anyone cared to offer him compensation or even an apology.

On a side note, a question worth further investigating is why no one bothered discussing whether the fact that he was innocent in both cases should mean that he would get back the right to carry a wand instead of using the lovely pretense of the pink umbrella.

4.4.4   Harry's Encounter with the Wizengamot

Last but not least, remember how Fudge had summoned the full Wizengamot when Harry had conjured the Patronus?

On the bright side—at least for once there was a trial. Taking every win we can get. But let's take a closer look at this trial.

Context for those who feel mildly confounded right now: Harry and Dudley had been on their way home in Little Whinging when two dementors appeared (sent by Dolores Umbridge, as was later revealed) and attacked Harry and his cousin. Harry then conjured a corporeal Patronus and chased away the dementors. As an immediate reaction, the Ministry of Magic expelled him from Hogwarts, only to then revoke the expulsion a few minutes later—after Dumbledore intervened. Harry then received another owl asking him to attend a disciplinary hearing given the charges of violating the Decree for the Reasonable Restriction of Underage Sorcery and the International Statute of Secrecy.[71]

Let's stop right here before we move on to any of the other questionable things that occurred. First, Harry was expulsed and then asked to attend a disciplinary hearing to determine whether he was actually guilty. If you want to paint a picture of lack of presumption of innocence, this is it. There was clearly a bias in favor of assuming that he was guilty, before Harry even set foot in the Ministry of Magic.

Now let's move on to the process itself. Let's repeat the conditions for a fair trial (I took the liberty to cross out the ones that don't seem to be of key concern):

---

[71]Rowling (2003), Chapter 2: A Peck of Owls.

- → ~~Tell people what they are accused of in a way and language they understand~~ · (the letter delivered by owl was as clear as it gets, one point for the Ministry of · Magic) ·
- → Give the person accused enough time to prepare their defense and talk to their · lawyer (whom they chose) (yeah – let's talk about that)
- → ~~Don't delay the trial~~ (not a problem, rather on the contrary – the Ministry of · Magic showed a real talent at speeding up the time of the hearing without · properly informing the accused)
- → Make sure that the accused is present during the trial and is able to either defend · themselves or be defended by a lawyer (whom they have to be able to choose · freely – and in case they can't afford, get financial support for) (another point · to talk about)
- → Allow the accused to bring their own witnesses (for their innocence) and · examine witnesses that accuse them (yep, another issue)
- → ~~Get support from an interpreter in case there are language issues~~
- → Not to testify against oneself or be asked to confess guilt (they really tried to get him to – good on him he didn't but definitely · an issue)

So let's take this one by one:

1) Time to Prepare Their Defense and Talk to His Lawyer

There are two aspects to this—time and ability to talk to a lawyer. In terms of time one might argue that the approximate 10 days between the attack and the hearing might not be enough. But there were no specific complaints about this, so let's just ignore it for now and assume this was sufficient for Harry to assess how to address this issue—not that he seemed to have done so in any meaningful way, given that he spent the time cleaning up 12 Grimmauld Place. The ability to talk to his lawyer is another interesting question. There was obviously no lawyer involved (which might also just be due to a lack of lawyers in the wizarding world).[72] Interestingly, Dumbledore appeared as Harry's witness for the defense (without Harry's knowledge or consent) and then acted as if he were Harry's lawyer. The fact that the two of them didn't talk prior to the trial did, however, not have anything to do with a lack of ability or the Ministry of Magic actively preventing it. Instead, it was due to the fact that Dumbledore feared that Voldemort would misuse his ability as a legilimens to possess Harry and gain valuable insights into the Order of the Phoenix and Dumbledore's plans. So while it would be great to add this to the "let's blame the Ministry of Magic" list, it does not seem like an ideal fit.

---

[72] Gava and Paterson (2010), p. 11.

2) Presence During Trial and Ability to Defend Himself or Be Defended by Lawyer

On to the next question then. Presence during the trial and ability to defend oneself or be defended.[73] We know that Harry was present during the trial and Dumbledore acted as his lawyer, of sorts. Yet, this is not a result of the efforts of the Ministry of Magic to ensure a fair trial. Quite to the contrary. The Ministry had actually changed the time and place of the hearing so that both Harry and Dumbledore would almost have missed the hearing. The fact that they managed to show up on time was more due to healthy caution about being on time from Arthur Weasley as well as due to Dumbledore's skepticism linked to all things Ministry of Magic during that phase. In total, this will be a balancing act. Yes, Harry was able to be present during the trial and was defended by Dumbledore, which is as good as it seems to get in the wizarding world. If the Ministry of Magic would have had its wishes, this would not have happened. But given the ironclad principle of voting in favor of the accused in case you are in doubt, let's assume that this right was not violated (and yes, the principle I'm referring to is *in dubio pro reo*).

3) Bring Own Witnesses

Now that we have established that Harry was able to be present and be defended by Dumbledore, let's move on to the question about whether he was able to bring his own witnesses. Again, this is an interesting situation in which there is a discrepancy between what the Ministry of Magic would have wanted and what materialized. In an ideal scenario, this right would be granted by officially informing the accused that they are allowed to bring their own witnesses to establish a case for their defense. This clearly did not happen here. As you might remember, there was a lot of confusion when Dumbledore announced that he would want to bring in a witness, Ms. Figg. The Ministry of Magic had clearly not envisioned this. Yet, they also did not actively prevent Ms. Figg from testifying. As Dumbledore had pointed out, under the Wizengamot Charter of Rights (yes, this seems to exist but given previous examples to lack of trials for Sirius and Hagrid we should really take a look at what it entails) the accused has the right to present witnesses for his or her case. This statement from Dumbledore was also confirmed by Madam Bones as official policy of the Department of Magical Law Enforcement.[74]

Once Ms. Figg was on the stand, the questions were clearly asked in a biased way. But, luckily for Harry, did not manage to persuade every member of the Wizengamot of the lack of credibility of the story. So yes, Harry was essentially able to bring his own witness. He might not have known about it, he was certainly not prepared for it, but it happened. So let's just go with this as a win for justice, not as one of the core issues to highlight.

---

[73] Kälin and Künzli (2010), p. 455.
[74] Rowling (2003), Chapter 8: The Hearing.

4) Not to Testify Against Oneself or Be Asked to Confess Guilt

On to the last question. Was Harry forced to testify against himself? Well, they certainly tried. Many of the questions that in particular Fudge asked were leading, to say the least. Yet, Harry always managed—luckily with the support from Dumbledore—to tell his part of the story rather than making a false confession of his guilt. While the intent from Fudge and Umbridge was clearly there, the process itself managed to reveal the truth rather than a false confession of guilt without hearing more about the reasons behind Harry's use of magic.

5) So This Was All Fair Game?

I know what you'll think—so this was all ok? No harm, no foul? Yes, essentially in this case it holds true. While the entire hearing felt off, starting with the fact that they convened the entire Wizengamot for this type of hearing, there is no clear indicator that any of Harry's rights were violated and that he was negatively impacted. Remember our checklist from earlier—if there was no harm inflicted, there is also no violation of a human right. There might have been the intent from the Ministry of Magic to violate the right to a fair trial. And as we have seen earlier, they certainly have a solid track record in doing so. Yet, in this specific case, there was no harm and therefore also no violation of the right to a fair trial.

4.4.5   Why Not Use Veritaserum or Legilimens?

Now on to the most obvious question that will come to mind: why are they not relying on *veritaserum* or *legilimens* instead of hoping for bogus confessions. Also not all that easy. Veritaserum seems appealing, yet it works best on the unsuspecting. Very skilled wizards and witches are able to avoid its effects by using antidotes, charms or occlumency. So while it might increase the likelihood of getting to the truth with some witches and wizards, the most evil ones will likely not be impressed if you pour the clear liquid into their tea. And it's not as if there were no situations in which *veritaserum* was used—or in which someone tried to use it. Just remember when Dolores Umbridge tried to force the truth about Dumbledore's whereabouts out of Harry or when Dumbledore used the *veritaserum* on Barty Crouch Jr.[75] As for *legilimens* this comes with the same challenge as *veritaserum*. Highly skilled witches and wizards will be able to use occlumency to shield their minds. Again, it might increase the likelihood of convicting some but then we'd also face the challenge of difference in treatment depending on skill level. And of course the obvious issues that you would make people testify against themselves (classic self-incrimination).[76]

---

[75] More on this in Barton (2010), pp. 33–34.

[76] More on why self-incrimination is not legal: Kälin and Künzli (2010), p. 458. The equivalent to *veritaserum* (although not as accurate) are lie detector tests. But even those are no longer admissible

4.5 Freedom from Torture in the Wizarding World: From Dementors to Umbridge

4.5.1 How Do We Define Torture?

Freedom from torture is considered *jus cogens*. In case you've been asleep throughout the first chapters, this means that every state has to uphold it. There is no claiming "I didn't ratify the treaty". But what do we understand as torture?

There are, again, as always, multiple treaties that prohibit torture. These include. Art. 5 Universal Declaration of Human Rights, Art. 7 ICCPR, CAT, Art. 3 ECHR, Art. 3 GC and many, many more. We'll stop here. If you want the full list, check out the footnotes.[77]

Art. 1 CAT

1. For the purposes of this Convention, the term "torture" means any act by which severe pain or suffering, whether physical or mental, is intentionally inflicted on a person for such purposes as obtaining from him or a third person information or a confession, punishing him for an act he or a third person has committed or is suspected of having committed, or intimidating or coercing him or a third person, or for any reason based on discrimination of any kind, when such pain or suffering is inflicted by or at the instigation of or with the consent or acquiescence of a public official or other person acting in an official capacity. It does not include pain or suffering arising only from, inherent in or incidental to lawful sanctions.

Let's take a closer look at what Art. 1 CAT tells us about the elements of torture. We have the following core elements:

- Severe pain or suffering, whether physical or mental
- Purpose: to obtain information or a confession, to punish, intimidate or coerce
- Inflicted by (or at least with consent of) public official or someone else acting in official capacity

One important aspect to note before we move on—many of the regional treaties and also the ICCPR are less restrictive in their definition of torture. In particular, they do not limit torture to acts inflicted by public officials or someone acting in an official

---

in court, meaning you can't just take out your lie detector, wait for the answer and convict based on that. More in: Stroud (2015).

[77] Treaties including the prohibition of torture are: Art. 5 Universal Declaration of Human Rights; Art. 7 ICCPR; CAT; OPCAT; Art. 37 CRC; Art. 15 CRPD; Art. 5 ACHR; Art. 5 ACHPR; Art. 8 ArCHR; Art. 3 ECHR; Art. 3 GC; Articles 13–14, 17, 87, 89 and 99 GC III; Articles 27, 31–32, 37, 100 and 118 f GC IV, Articles 11 and 75 AP I; Art. 4 AP II, Art. 7 (1) f and 2 e and Art. 8 (2) a ii and c Rome Statue. More in Kälin and Künzli (2010), p. 321.

capacity. We will keep the following section to the definition of torture based on Art. 1 CAT (not because I am lazy, but in particular as the core cases we want to look at in the wizarding world all tie back to acts of the government). But bear in mind that there is more to torture if you move beyond the CAT definition.

The different treaties that forbid torture also forbid inhuman or degrading treatment or punishment. First step for us is therefore to understand when we are talking about torture vs. any of the others. There are two ways of approaching this. One is to assess the intensity of the suffering, the other one is to assess the purpose of the abuse. As lawyers have the incredible urge to name every theory there is, you'll find more information on this under the titles of the "degree of severity theory" as well as the "purpose theory".[78] It's as straight forward as it sounds. Under the "degree of severity theory" you assess how extreme the pain inflicted is. Under the "purpose theory" the core factor to assess is whether the pain or suffering was inflicted to reach a specific goal.

Now let's take the proverbial step back. Does it make any difference whether an act is qualified as torture or inhuman and degrading treatment or punishment? Not really. It would still be a violation of the same articles in the different treaties. So let's just keep it simple—there has to be pain or suffering. It can be physical or mental.[79] But does this mean that basically any act could qualify as torture or inhuman or degrading treatment or punishment? Of course not. Common sense often times helps answer legal questions—just don't tell the lawyers that it is not always that complicated. There needs to be a minimum degree of intensity.

Now what does minimum degree of intensity mean? It depends on the circumstances.[80] These can include the duration of the treatment, the mental and physical effects it has, the individual and so on. We'll look at different cases in detail to understand whether this would qualify as torture.

4.5.2 Dementors at Azkaban

Let us start with the most obvious case: the use of dementors in Azkaban. Yes, you will roll your eyes and shake your heads that we even attempt to discuss this. Of course it is torture. But trials in our world don't work like this. You always have to establish proof. Call it overcomplicated or a protection of the innocent. So let us take a look at the three conditions for torture as laid out in Art. 1 CAT.

First, we need to test whether the act itself causes pain or suffering. Well, yes. Dementors suck out every happy memory of the prisoners and they can go mad within weeks in Azkaban.[81] Having the feeling that you will never be happy again in your life and not only for a short period of time, but the entire duration of your

---

[78] More on this in Kälin and Künzli (2010), pp. 322 ff.

[79] Kälin and Künzli (2010), p. 322.

[80] Kälin and Künzli (2010), pp. 329–330.

[81] Rowling (1999), Chapter 10: The Marauder's Map.

sometimes lifelong stay in Azkaban, certainly meets that threshold of mental harm. If this wouldn't, what would?

Second, we need to understand the purpose of this infliction of harm. In case of the dementors in Azkaban it is quite straightforward. It is about punishing the inmates of Azkaban for the crimes they (allegedly) did commit and weakening them to the point where escape becomes impossible. So we also get a 10/10 on the purpose side.

Finally, the pain has to be "inflicted by or at the instigation of or with the consent or acquiescence of a public official or other person acting in an official capacity". Again, quite straightforward. The dementors are on official mission at Azkaban. They are charged with keeping the prisoners in Azkaban. The Ministry of Magic is aware of this, fully understanding the consequences, and is consenting to it. Does it matter that we are not quite sure what dementors actually are? Not really. Whether they are considered as subjects of the law themselves (like human beings) or as trained beasts that do the bidding of their "owner", the state officials placing them in charge of guarding and abusing the prisoners would have committed torture.

So in a nutshell, yes, this is as clear a case of torture as you can find. It changes from the moment on when Voldemort orders the dementors to join him in his cause and they leave Azkaban. Then, the strict definition of Art. 1 CAT no longer applies up until the point when Voldemort and his death eaters take over the Ministry of Magic. Yet, until then, there was a prolonged torture case that would urgently need to be tackled in front of the WCHR, if one were to exist.

4.5.3   Dementor's Kiss of Barty Crouch Jr.

Let us now look at something that is even worse than just having every happy memory sucked out of you—the dementor's kiss. The dementor's kiss sucks out the victim's soul and leaves only an empty shell that has no memory or personality.[82]

The dementor's kiss was performed on Barty Crouch Jr. with consent from Fudge.[83] Again, there was no process at all. So let's not even pretend to discuss a fair trial for Barty Crouch Jr. There was no trial. But instead of going into a rant on how this is a huge no no, let me focus on assessing whether—on top of the violation of the right to a fair trial—Fudge also managed to get full points for torture through this act.

First, yes, there is obviously severe pain and suffering. Having your soul sucked out not only sounds painful (and looks painful based on how it is depicted), it is also inflicting the severest possible form of mental harm. Second, the purpose was clearly to punish Barty Crouch Jr. for his acts. In addition to this, it also saved Fudge the political embarrassment of the full statement of Barty Crouch Jr. Lastly, yes, it was

---

[82] More on this in Schwabach (2010), pp. 81–82.

[83] Details of this horrific incident in: Rowling (2000), Chapter 36: The Parting of the Ways.

done with consent from a public official—the Minister of Magic himself. To conclude this—yes, it was clearly an act of torture.

4.5.4   Umbridge and Her Special Quill

Another clear candidate for a torture conviction is our all-time favorite Dolores Umbridge. Let's for a brief moment ignore the fact that she—allegedly—sent dementors to finish off Harry during his summer break and only focus on her activities while on official mission at Hogwarts. As you might recall, Professor Umbridge had a unique teaching approach, in particular in punishing students who had the nerve to speak up or contradict her in class.

Using her particularly nasty quill, she made students, including Harry, write the line "I must not tell lies" on a sheet of paper. Instead of ink, the quill was writing in blood and left an ever-deepening scar on the back of the hand of Harry and the other unfortunate students affected by this. Let's go through the motion again and test the three conditions for torture as laid out in Art. 1 CAT.

First, the lasting scar on the students' hands clearly presents severe pain and suffering. One might have argued during the first class when there was only pain but no lasting damage (though even then it would have been borderline), but especially after the scar appeared, there is no argument to be made. Second, the pain was inflicted with the specific purpose to punish those students who dared speak up. Lastly, we have to assess whether Prof. Umbridge was acting as a public official or in official capacity. This could be a tricky question if she would have been purely a professor at Hogwarts—although even in this case Hogwarts can be seen as a public institution and her position would have been sufficient.[84] Yet, in our case, it is very straightforward as she was also acting as Inquisitor at Hogwarts on Fudge's orders. We will therefore be able to assume that there is link to her official capacity. To conclude, all requirements for torture under Art. 1 CAT are given in Umbridge's case.

4.5.5   The Carrows and the Cruciatus Bootcamp

On to another case example—the Carrows. Here, there are two distinct cases to consider. First, Amycus Carrow, who was teaching the Dark Arts class during what would have been Harry's 7th year at Hogwarts, required his students to practice the *Cruciatus* Curse on other students who had received detention. Second, Amycus and his sibling also used the curse on students as they saw fit. When testing whether this meets the requirements for torture, we again face quite a simple case linked to the first requirement. The *Cruciatus* Curse literally means the Torture Curse and inflicts severe pain and suffering. This can even lead to complete insanity, as happened with

---

[84] More on the status of Hogwarts right in the next section: Sect. 4.5.5.

Neville's parents. The pain was inflicted with the clear goal to punish those who had earned detention or who were not acting as the Carrows envisioned (mainly members of Dumbledore's Army). The last question is a bit more tricky here and ties back to the question of whether professors at a school are considered state officials.

Let's first try to understand the status of Hogwarts to understand the status of the Carrows as potential government officials—is Hogwarts a public or private school? We don't really have that level of visibility when it comes to Hogwarts (yes, we discussed this before—core points are repeated here to make your life easier).[85] In some instances it seems as though Hogwarts is a private school, given the level of autonomy that Dumbledore enjoys. In other instances, there is heavy government involvement. This includes not only Umbridge's role as Inquisitor but also the role of the Board of Governors. The 12 witches and wizards of the Board of Governors have the right to inspect and even shut down the school. All this clearly points to the status of Hogwarts as a public institution.

And even if some of you are not convinced, international law is there to save us from a deep dive into the status of Hogwarts. When we look at what the duty to respect entails, states cannot simply avoid responsibility by privatizing a task. Instead, states are responsible for human rights violations if staff or private schools or private prisons torture those they are in control of. In our case, this therefore means that even if we consider Hogwarts a private school, the acts of the Carrows would be considered torture under Art. 1 CAT.[86]

Linked to the Carrows, it is even easier than that. After Voldemort took over the Ministry of Magic, the death eaters also seized control over Hogwarts, instated themselves as professors (e.g., our lovely Carrows) and made enrollment mandatory. So yes, in this very year we can consider Hogwarts very much a public school and the Carrows therefore state officials. This also means that all requirements for torture under Art. 1 CAT are fulfilled in this case.

Interestingly, the *Cruciatus Curse*—along the other two previously Unforgivable Curses—was legalized when Voldemort took over the Ministry of Magic. The Carrows were therefore not per se acting illegally by practicing the curses. This, of course, only holds true if we follow wizarding law. If they were subject to Muggle law, there would be no way that torturing students would be ok. This again is a perfect example that states can derogate and opt out of certain rights, but not all. Torture is one of those where no excuses are allowed that would make it legal for you to pursue it.[87]

---

[85] If you wonder where you read it, please go back to Sect. 3.5.

[86] Kälin and Künzli (2010), pp. 333–334.

[87] More on this in Sect. 1.4.

4.5.6 Harry Torturing a Hogwarts Professor

To ensure that everyone gets off their high horse ("typical of the death eaters to torture"): even our hero Harry has done so. Remember when he entered Hogwarts in search of another horcrux and encountered Amycus Carrow who spat into Professor McGonagall's face? Harry used the *Cruciatus Curse* to punish Amycus Carrow until he smashed into a bookcase and became unconscious.[88] Clearly meeting the severe pain and suffering threshold and also clearly done in order to punish for the act of disrespect.[89] In Harry's case we will not be able to link this to an official capacity— therefore, the only relevant torture convictions that could be achieved would be linked to him acting in a private capacity.

Same as in the case of the Carrows, the added complication is that at the time when Harry used the curse, it was considered legal based on Ministry of Magic guidance. Purely under wizarding law, this was therefore unproblematic. It would be different if Harry were subject to Muggle law.

The situation when he intended to torture Bellatrix would be different. But in that situation—as Bellatrix explained to him—he didn't really mean to use the curse.[90] So even attempted torture would be difficult to prove.

4.6 Does the Aurors' Use of the Unforgivable Curses Violate Human Rights?

4.6.1 Violation of Human Rights by State Agents

Let us briefly turn away from the wizarding world and towards our world. Imagine reading in the newspaper about a hostage crisis and the police shooting the hostage taker to free the hostages. Just for the sake of argument, let us assume that shooting the hostage taker was the only way out. There was no other option to guarantee the survival of the hostages. Should the police officer go to jail for this?

While we have not talked about the right to life in detail, I hope you are aware of its existence. Given that there is such a thing as a right to life, it seems odd at first that a state official (which a police officer is in every case) would be allowed to violate this right. But it also seems odd to ask a state official to let innocent people die because he was unable or unwilling to act or afraid to go to jail for his actions.

It is important to understand that human rights are rarely absolute. What does that mean? There are exceptions. These exceptions depend on the relevant right. There are different exceptions when it comes to the right to life and the prohibition of torture. We will look at those linked to the relevant unforgivable curses.

---

[88] If you want to read up on this, go to Rowling (2007), Chapter 30: The Sacking of Severus Snape.
[89] More on this in: Schwabach (2010), p. 69.
[90] Rowling (2003), Chapter 36: The Only One He Ever Feared.

Now why do we want to look at this? Essentially, we need to understand whether it is ok that the Aurors are using unforgivable curses. We will take a look at our world to understand if there are any lessons that can be applied to the wizarding world, fully conscious of the difficulty that we don't really know whether we should equate the Aurors more with the regular police, SWAT teams or anti-terrorist units.[91]

4.6.2   Violation Through the Aurors' Use of Unforgivable Curses

The three Unforgivable Curses are (1) the *Imperius* Curse, (2) the *Cruciatus* Curse and (3) the *Killing Curse*. They were classified as Unforgivable in 1717.[92] The first allows the user to control the victim's actions, the second causes unbearable pain and the third kills the victim instantly. The use of these curses leads to life imprisonment in Azkaban.

The **Imperius Curse** enables others to control the victim's actions. It was for example used by Draco Malfoy on Madam Rosmerta, by the death eaters on Pius Thicknesse, and by the Moody impersonator Barty Crouch Jr. on his Defence against the Dark Arts class during Harry's 4th year at Hogwarts.

To remind ourselves—the goal is not to debate the pros and cons of using the *Imperius* Curse. Our goal is to understand if there are circumstances in which it is ok that the Aurors, acting as state officials, are using this unforgivable curse on anyone.

There is no direct equivalent to the *Imperius* Curse in the Muggle world. Indeed, this will greatly depend on what the victim is made to do. Consider if the victim of the *Imperius* Curse is made to stay at home for an extended period of time (think about Barty Crouch Jr. being made to stay at home after he was rescued from Azkaban). In that case, we would have to check for restrictions on the freedom of movement. In case this is done by a state official, it will likely be justifiable if the victim was trying to commit a crime and could be most easily prevented from doing so by placing them under the *Imperius* Curse—of course, the final assessment depends on what the person is made to do under the *Imperius* Curse. It would be different if the victims of the *Imperius* Curse were made to harm themselves. In that case, we would need to check whether there is a justification for the infliction of bodily harm. Less likely though, given that if one decides to use the *Imperius* Curse, it is fully possible to limit the impact to restraining a person rather than making that person hurt themself. If the person is just made to sing a song and therefore cannot curse anyone else at the same time, this likely will be justifiable given the limited negative impact on the individual compared to the potential negative impact of that person cursing others. So yes, there are situations in which it seems justifiable to place someone under the *Imperius* Curse.

---

[91] Basing this analogy on Gava and Paterson (2010), p. 10.

[92] Professor Dumbledore's Notes in: The Tales of Beedle the Bard, p. 84.

On to the *Cruciatus* **Curse**. As mentioned before, this is the Torture Curse. The question is therefore whether in any situations torture committed by state officials can be justified. Torture is a special human right given the absolute nature of the prohibition. Sounds fancy but what does "absolute nature of the prohibition" mean? It means: no exceptions. You cannot torture. Ever. This is affirmed in Art. 2 CAT and also highlighted in IHL—meaning that you cannot even torture during an armed conflict. It does not matter whether torturing someone could lead to you saving the lives of third parties in case of terrorist threats (the so-called "ticking time bomb scenario").[93] There are no exceptions. This also means that for the Aurors the *Cruciatus* Curse would have to be fully off limits. Spinning this further: if Harry were subject to Muggle jurisdiction, he would have gone to jail for torturing Amycus Carrow. Luckily for him, the curses were legalized when Voldemort had taken over the Ministry of Magic. There was therefore no prosecution of Harry for the use of the *Cruciatus* Curse. But if we were to follow Muggle legal logic, this could not have happened.

To understand whether the use of *Avada Kedavra* by the Aurors violates the right to life, we need to understand whether there are any situations under which Muggle law enables state officials (in particular the police) to kill another human being without going to jail for it. Art. 6 (1) ICCPR will help us understand this further. It explicitly prohibits the "arbitrary" deprivation of human life. Art. 2 ECHR is even more helpful to understand the distinction.

Art. 2 ECHR

1. Everyone's right to life shall be protected by law. No one shall be deprived of his life intentionally save in the execution of a sentence of a court following his conviction of a crime for which this penalty is provided by law.
2. Deprivation of life shall not be regarded as inflicted in contravention of this article when it results from the use of force which is no more than absolutely necessary:
   (a) in defence of any person from unlawful violence;
   (b) in order to effect a lawful arrest or to prevent the escape of a person lawfully detained;
   (c) in action lawfully taken for the purpose of quelling a riot or insurrection.

Now we are getting a bit closer to what this is all about. A police officer shooting someone is not considered a violation of Art. 2 ECHR if it is linked to defending a person from unlawful violence, to prevent the escape of a person or if it is linked to

---

[93] More on the absolute nature of the prohibition of torture: Kälin and Künzli (2010), p. 333. More on the use of unforgivable curses: Schwabach (2010), pp. 443–452. If you are interested in this topic, there is also a very fascinating case linked to the abduction of a child and a police officer threatening to torture the suspect to find out the child's location. In the end, the ECHR found that threatening to use torture even if done to save a child's life is unlawful. More on tis in *Gäfgen v. Germany*, 22978/05, Judgment, 3 June 2010.

quelling a riot or insurrection.[94] In our case linked to the hostage taker, shooting that person could be justified given that it was done in defence of another person from unlawful violence.

Now what does this mean for the Aurors? Can they just go around throwing the *Killing Curse* at every suspected death eater? Well, they shouldn't. But there are scenarios in which they could get away with it, even if facing stricter Muggle jurisdiction post their action. There will be different scenarios. In the case of the death eaters attacking Harry and his friends in the Ministry of Magic, the use of force by anyone coming to Harry's help can be justified, given that it aims to defend another person from unlawful violence. In the case of Aurors hunting down known and convicted death eaters who escaped Azkaban (e.g., Bellatrix Lestrange), it would also be legal given that it is linked to making a lawful arrest.[95]

When it comes to hunting down suspected death eaters it will depend very much on the specific circumstances. If the suspected death eater does not attack first or threaten anyone in that particular situation, the Auror will not be allowed to use the *Killing Curse* solely to prevent the suspect from escaping. Yet, given that it is almost a given that the death eaters will be carrying their wand and therefore something comparable to a weapon for Muggles (given their likely way of using it), Aurors will at least have a likely excuse in case there was no way to prevent the use of the *Killing Curse*.[96]

4.7   How Can Human Rights Help Against House-Elf Enslavement?

4.7.1   Prohibition of Slavery

The original definition of slavery refers to the ownership of individuals and the exploitation of those individuals by their "owners".

Art. 8 ICCPR

1. No one shall be held in slavery; slavery and slave-trade in all their forms shall be prohibited.
2. Not one shall be held in servitude.

Under the Rome Statute, slavery is defined as "the exercise of any or all of the powers attaching to the right of ownership over a person includ[ing] the exercise of such power in the course of trafficking in persons, in particular women and

---

[94]It is of course a bit more complicated than I highlighted here—to get the full sense of the complexity, please refer to Kälin and Künzli (2010), pp. 276 ff.

[95]Refer to Kälin and Künzli (2010), p. 275 for more details on lawful arrests and arbitrary killings.

[96]More details on the legal cases before the ECtHR that discussed exactly these questions: Kälin and Künzli (2010), pp. 275 ff.

children".[97] Slavery has been outlawed worldwide. Yet, some practices that amount to exploitation of human beings unfortunately still exist. This includes human trafficking for economic exploitation, forced recruitment of child soldiers or enforced prostitution. Given that it is mainly private individuals or institutions who violate the prohibition of slavery nowadays (yes, there are some notable exceptions, but we will leave politics out of this for now), states have to focus on their duty to protect. This means that there needs to be legislation prohibiting modern forms of slavery and victims need to be given the chance to go to court and complain about any violations that occurred.[98]

4.7.2   What Are House-Elves?

House-elves are magical creatures "bound to serve one house and one family [of wizards] forever".[99] They keep the family's secrets and loyally serve it for their entire life. They have completely lost sight of their rights and are only speaking about themselves in the third persona, hurt themselves when disobeying their masters and are confused once they are treated as equals.[100]

4.7.3   Are House-Elves Enslaved?

Well, at first sight, the answer is clearly yes. House-elves speak of themselves as an enslaved species. They are owned by their masters who exert complete control over them. They can only be freed by their master if they are given clothes. They don't earn any income with their work, with a few exceptions later on in the books starting with Dobby.[101] Instead, they are treated like property. Some families even severely mistreat their housel-elves. The Black family has started a tradition of beheading house-elves when they got too old to carry tea trays.[102] But does this mean that they are enslaved?

The challenge will be whether house-elves could qualify for protection under a Muggle treaty. Technically, house-elves are not human but humanoid creatures. They are therefore not protected under the Muggle prohibition against enslavement. In addition, there is limited chance for anyone brining a court case on house-elf enslavement to a Muggle court. Yet another reason to establish a WCHR that would also have a mandate to deal with house-elf enslavement, following similar

---

[97] Art. 7 (2) lit. c Rome Statute.

[98] More on this in: Kälin and Künzli (2010), pp. 421–423.

[99] Rowling (1998), Chapter 2: Dobby's Warning.

[100] Rowling (1998), Chapter 2: Dobby's Warning.

[101] On Dobby's negotiation of a contract, please see Rowling (2000), Chapter 21: The House-Elf Liberation Front.

[102] Rowling (2003), Chapter 6: The Noble and Most Ancient House of Black.

definitions as Muggles do. If they were human, the treatment of house-elves would constitute a violation of the prohibition of slavery.

4.7.4 A Critical Evaluation of S.P.E.W.

This now leads us to Hermione's Society for the Promotion of Elfish Welfare (S.P.E. W.). The organization's goal was to enable house-elves to have fair wages and working conditions as well as ensuring representation in the Department for the Regulation and Control of Magical Creatures.[103] While the intent was certainly noble, there was a clear challenge linked to the initiatives of S.P.E.W. When Hermione started leaving her hats all over the place to free the house-elves, the majority of the house-elves at Hogwarts (technically all but Dobby) felt insulted and refused to clean the Gryffindor common room. This left only Dobby cleaning the common room, which was certainly not what Hermione had intended. This episode highlights challenges that can come with activism if it is purely driven on behalf of a third party rather than involving that third party and thereby creating ownership.

References

Barton BH (2010) Harry Potter and the half-crazed bureaucracy. In: Thomas JE, Snyder FG (eds) The law and Harry Potter. Carolina Academic Press, Durham, pp 33–47

Bowcott O (2014) The European court of human rights' judgements that transformed British law. The Guardian. https://www.theguardian.com/law/2014/oct/03/landmarks-human-rights-echr-judgments-transformed-british-law. Accessed 20 Dec 2022

da Costa K (2013) The extraterritorial application of selected human rights treaties. Martinus Nijhoff, Leiden

de Wolf AH (2012) Reconciling privatization with human rights. Intersentia, Cambridge

Dundes Renteln A (1990) International human rights: universalism versus relativism. Sage Publications, Newbury Park

Gava J, Paterson JM (2010) What role need law play in a society with magic? In: Thomas JE, Snyder FG (eds) The law and Harry Potter. Carolina Academic Press, Durham, pp 3–16

Kälin W, Künzli J (2010) The law of international human rights protection. Oxford University Press, Oxford

Keaten J (2022) UN Human Rights Council rejects western bid to debate China's Xinjiang abuses. The Diplomat. https://thediplomat.com/2022/10/un-human-rights-council-rejects-western-bid-to-debate-chinas-xinjiang-abuses/. Accessed 20 Dec 2022

Kolb R (2017) The international law of state responsibility: an introduction. Edward Elgar, Cheltenham

Murphy M (2022) France must reconsider ban on IS members' return. BBC. https://www.bbc.com/news/world-europe-62905237. Accessed 20 Dec 2022

OHCHR (2022a) Complaint procedure – FAQ. https://www.ohchr.org/EN/HRBodies/HRC/ComplaintProcedure/Pages/FAQ.aspx. Accessed 20 Dec 2022

---

[103] Rowling (2000), Chapter 14: The Unforgivable Curses.

OHCHR (2022b) The core international human rights instruments and their monitoring bodies. https://www.ohchr.org/EN/ProfessionalInterest/Pages/CoreInstruments.aspx.   Accessed 20 Dec 2022

OHCHR (2022c) Human Rights Council complaint procedure. https://www.ohchr.org/en/hr-bodies/hrc/complaint-procedure/hrc-complaint-procedure-index. Accessed 20 Dec 2020

Panikkar R (1982) Is the notion of human rights a western concept? Diogenes 30:75–102

Rapp GC (2010) Sirius black: a case study in actual innocence. In: Thomas JE, Snyder FG (eds) The law and Harry Potter. Carolina Academic Press, Durham, pp 91–101

Renz F (2020) State responsibility and new trends in the privatization of warfare. Edward Elgar, Northampton

Rowling JK (1998) Harry Potter and the chamber of secrets. Bloomsbury, London

Rowling JK (1999) Harry Potter and the prisoner of Azkaban. Bloomsbury, London

Rowling JK (2000) Harry Potter and the goblet of fire. Bloomsbury, London

Rowling JK (2003) Harry Potter and the order of the phoenix. Bloomsbury, London

Rowling JK (2007) Harry Potter and the deathly hallows. Bloomsbury, London

Schwabach A (2010) Harry Potter and the unforgivable curses. In: Thomas JE, Snyder FG (eds) The law and Harry Potter. Carolina Academic Press, Durham, pp 67–90

Shaw MN (2017) International law, 8th edn. Cambridge University Press, Cambridge

Stroud M (2015) Will lie detectors ever get their day in court again? Bloomberg. https://www.bloomberg.com/news/articles/2015-02-02/will-lie-detectors-ever-get-their-day-in-court-again-?leadSource=uverify%20wall. Accessed 20 Dec 2022

Trechsel S (2005) The right to a public hearing. In: Trechsel S, Summers S (eds) Human rights in criminal proceedings. Oxford University Press, Oxford, pp 117–133

UN (2022). https://ask.un.org/loader?fid=11125&type=1&key=6bf400a0db526933d8577cce49f39ad2. Accessed 30 Jan 2022

Watson GR (2010) The persecution of Tom Riddle: a study in human rights law. In: Thomas JE, Snyder F (eds) The law and Harry Potter. Carolina Academic Press, Durham, pp 103–118

Weissbrodt D (2014) International fair trial guarantees. In: Clapham A, Gaeta P (eds) The Oxford handbook of international law in armed conflict, pp 410–440

Zvobgo K, Sandholtz W, Mulesky S (2020) Reserving rights: explaining human rights treaty reservations. Int Stud Q 64:785–797

International Criminal Law

5

Abstract

Now that you have been immersed into the world of human rights law and law of armed conflict, one big question remains—how can those who violate legal norms be held accountable? Is there a way that Voldemort and the death eaters could be brought to justice? We will take a look at the international court system to assess whether this would be sufficient to hold criminals from the wizarding world responsible for their crimes.

5.1   What Do We Mean by International Criminal Law?

International criminal law aims to hold individuals responsible for serious violations of international law. This branch of law is explicitly not targeted at states but only individuals. It started out post World War II during the Nuremberg and Tokyo tribunals where individuals were prosecuted for the atrocities they had committed. There is a limited number of crimes that can be prosecuted in the context of international criminal law. Everything else is subject to national criminal law. The crimes that can be prosecuted are war crimes, crimes against humanity, genocide and aggression.

There are several courts in charge of implementing international criminal law. It starts out with national legal systems (e.g., military tribunals or regular courts). If they are unable or unwilling to conduct the trial, the case might be heard in front of an ad hoc tribunal, an internationalized tribunal or the ICC. Important courts and tribunals to know are the ICTY, ICTR and the ICC.

The ICTY was established in 1993 through a resolution of the UNSC.[1] It had jurisdiction over grave breaches of the GC, violations of the laws or customs of war, genocide and crimes against humanity committed on the territory of the former

---

[1] Resolution 827 of UNSC.

Yugoslavia since 1991. The last judgment of the ICTY was issued in November 2017 and it ceased to exist in December 2017. Since then, oversight of sentences and any remaining appeal proceedings are dealt with under the International Residual Mechanism for Criminal Tribunals (IRMCT).[2]

The ICTR was established in 1994, also through a resolution of the UNSC.[3] It had jurisdiction over all acts linked to Rwandan genocide, crimes against humanity and violations of common Art. 3 GC I-IV and AP II of the GC in Rwanda, or by Rwandan citizens in nearby states throughout 1994. The IRMCT took over from 2017 on.[4]

In 1998, the Rome Statute was signed and in 2002 the ICC established. It is a permanent international court and has jurisdiction over the crimes of genocide, crimes against humanity, war crimes and crime of aggression. Currently, there are 123 member states (the UN has 193 in total). Several states, including the United States, China and Russia, have either not signed or not become parties to the Rome Statute.[5] Yes, that is as bad as it sounds. We will look at the jurisdiction of the ICC in more detail later.[6] But the difficulty is that it can only investigate and prosecute if the crime was committed within a member state, by a national of a member state or if the situation was referred to the ICC by the UNSC. Any observant reader among you will now look up the composition of the UN Security Council (UNSC) and realize that with the U.S., China and Russia three out of the five veto powers did not ratify the Rome Statute. Yes, this is a bummer. But there were still several important arrests to celebrate. So, let's focus on the positive for now, there is plenty of negativity going around already.

5.2   Are the Death Eaters Committing Genocide?

5.2.1   What Are Criteria for Genocide?

Art. 6 Rome Statute

For the purpose of this Statute, "genocide" means any of the following acts committed with intent to destroy, in whole or in part, a national, ethnical, racial or religious group, as such:

a) Killing members of the group;
b) Causing serious bodily or mental harm to members of the group;

---

[2] More background on the ICTY in: Shaw (2017), pp. 292 ff.

[3] Resolution 955 of UNSC.

[4] For more on the ICTR refer to: Shaw (2017), pp. 295 ff.

[5] To see the latest status of ratifications of the Rome Statue: https://asp.icc-cpi.int/states-parties.

[6] If you want to take a sneak peak, look here: Sect. 5.6.

c) Deliberately inflicting on the group conditions of life calculated to bring about its physical destruction in whole or in part;
d) Imposing measures intended to prevent births within the group;
e) Forcibly transferring children of the group to another group.

Based on the definition in Art. 6 Rome Statute we will have to check for the following elements:

- The perpetrator committing any of the acts listed under letters a-e
- The victim belonging to a particular national, ethnic, racial or religious group and the perpetrator selects the victim based on the membership in this group
- A specific intent to destroy at least a substantial part of the group
- A pattern of similar acts directed against the same group or an act that in itself could destroy the group[7]

5.2.2 Does the Death Eaters Campaign Against Muggle-Borns and Halfbloods Qualify as Genocide?

The death eaters have quite the rap sheet. For this particular question, let us ignore all the other horrible things they have done and solely focus on their campaign against Muggles and Muggle-borns witches and wizards after their return into the open. We thereby limit the relevant time to the period between the fight in the Ministry of Magic to the Battle of Hogwarts.

5.2.2.1 Are the Death Eaters Committing Any of the Relevant Acts?
When we look at the list of acts that are listed in Art. 6 Rome Statute, the death eaters have committed quite a range of them. There are numerous instances of killings ever since Voldemort ensured the wizarding world of his return through his intrusion into the Ministry of Magic—after his death eaters tried to recover the prophecy.[8] There are also several instances of causing serious bodily or mental harm through torture. In addition to the individual acts by death eaters there were also the acts of the Muggle-Born Registration Commission that was set up by the Ministry of Magic once Voldemort had taken over. The Commission forced all Muggle-born witches and wizards to register and interrogated them on how they "stole their magical power". It was then used as a pretense for imprisoning Muggle-borns in Azkaban where many of them died. In short, yes, several of the required acts occurred during this phase.

---

[7] Kälin and Künzli (2010), pp. 299–300; Cassese and Gaeta (2013), pp. 109 ff.
[8] Rowling (2003), Chapter 36: The Only One He Ever Feared.

5.2.2.2 Are Muggle-Borns and Halfbloods a Protected Group?

We now need to understand whether Muggle-borns and halfbloods can be seen as a protected group. We are defining four groups as protected from genocide: national, ethnical, racial and religious groups. Other groups (linguistic groups, meaning people speaking one specific language; political groups, meaning people following a certain political ideology) were excluded from this definition.[9] When the international criminal courts discuss whether a group that is targeted by genocide-like acts is indeed a protected group, they typically use a mix of objective and subjective markers. These can be objective criteria such as physical appearances, religion or cultural practices. But it can also be subjective criteria such as whether the perpetrator thought the victim belonged to a protected group. There are, of course, many discussions among lawyers when it comes to the relevant criteria and the degree to which subjective markers can play a role. I'll spare you the details here (if you are like Hermione, please check out the many references below).[10]

Let's take a look at whether Muggle-borns witches and wizards or halfbloods might be such a protected group. Before jumping to any conclusions, it is important to understand the status of the different groups. In a nutshell, there are Muggles (those without magic abilities), Muggle-borns (those born to Muggle parents but with magic abilities), halfbloods (with one Muggle parent and one wizarding parent), pure-bloods (those with purely wizarding ancestry) and squibs (those born to wizarding parents but without magic abilities).

The concept of "pure-blood" families or individuals is associated with Salazar Slytherin. With the uncertainty around relations to Muggles following the adoption of the International Statute of Secrecy in 1692, the pure-blood doctrine gained more followers. Witches and wizards were forced to hide from the Muggle eyes and were pushed towards segregation. Some elements of those promoting the pure-blood doctrine sound similar to Nazi racial sciences,[11] that were aiming to find pseudo-scientific proof of the superiority of the Aryan race.[12]

These signs have, of course, no basis in facts. The "Pure-Blood Directory" published in the 1930s goes one step further and creates a list of the "Sacred Twenty-Eight" families considered truly pure-blood. Some of those families, such as the Weasleys, found themselves on this list, but highlighted that they have ancestral ties to many interesting Muggles.[13]

Halfbloods are wizards of mixed heritage. Famous examples are Professor McGonagall but also Voldemort himself (even though he clearly didn't like this

---

[9]Schabas (2009), p. 117. More details on the groups protected from genocide: Schabas (2009), pp. 124 ff.

[10]More details on protected groups: Shaw (2017), p. 317 f.; Kälin and Künzli (2010), p. 298; Maison (2010), pp. 95–119; Werle and Jeßberger (2020), Chapter Three.

[11]More on this in: Kälin and Künzli (2010), p. 298.

[12]Rowling (2015b).

[13]Rowling (2015b).

fact and would have preferred to ignore his Muggle father and namesake Tom Riddle).

Muggle-borns are purely from Muggle families. They are derogatorily called "Mudbloods" (as happened to Hermione when fighting with Draco Malfoy).

Squibs are born to wizarding parents but don't have any wizarding ability themselves. During "normal" times, witches and wizards enjoyed the same rights, irrespective of whether they were Muggle-born, halfblood or "pure-blood". This did, however, change when Voldemort and the death eaters took over. The goal of Voldemort's death eaters seemed to be to rid the wizarding community of all Muggle influence. But are these other groups considered protected groups?

Well, the groups certainly share objectively observable features—the ability to do magic. But what type of protected group would this fall under? National or religious groups don't make any sense. This leaves the option of racial or ethnic groups. Racial groups are often times defined as groups with hereditary physical traits that are associated with geographical regions. Ethnic groups are those sharing a common language or culture.[14] The only objectively observable common trait of Muggle-borns and halfblood witches and wizards is, as mentioned, their ability to do magic. They also, at least in part, share their own culture given the unique mix of insights into the Muggle and wizarding world. Without doubt, they were not the type of protected group that those codifying the crime of genocide had in mind. Yet, the list of protected groups is on purpose not set to a distinct list of groups, but is open to any group as long as it meets the requirements. The common trait shared by Muggle-borns and halfblood witches and wizards meets this criterion. They are therefore considered a protected group linked to the crime of genocide.

5.2.3 Death Eaters Intent to Destroy

Once the death eaters took over the Ministry of Magic, they made many drastic changes. One was that they started releasing propaganda claiming that magic can only be inherited, which is why Muggle-born witches and wizards must have stolen magic from "real" witches and wizards. The Muggle-Born Registration Commission was used as a front to convict Muggle-borns of theft and sentence them to Azkaban or stripping them of their wands, jobs and families. Especially the fact that they sent Muggle-borns to Azkaban is essential here. As we had previously highlighted, many of them died there and the rest were tortured given their presence in close proximity to the dementors.

There was limited secrecy around the intent behind the Muggle-born Registration Commission, as indicated in the Daily Prophet article that highlighted the fear of Muggle-borns having stolen magical power.[15]

---

[14]More on the definition of these groups in: Lingaas (2015).

[15]More in: Harry Potter Fandom (n.d.).

But is all of this sufficient to qualify as intent to destroy? The death eaters certainly aimed to rid the wizarding community of Muggle-born and half-blood witches and wizards, basically any who are not pure-bloods. Yet, this does not necessarily have to mean destroying the group. It could also mean that they are excluded from the wizarding world and forced to live among Muggles, disguising their magical ability.

The fact that there is the Muggle-born Registration Commission in place and Muggle-borns are sent off to Azkaban indicates that the goal is to rid society of these people completely, not just banning them from the wizarding world. As some examples from the Muggle world indicate, sending off entire ethnic or racial groups to prisons and claiming that they have committed crimes they did not commit is a phenomenon we see not only in the wizarding world.

5.2.4 Yes, This Seems Like Attempted Genocide

To summarize: all criteria are given, the death eaters are carrying out the relevant acts,[16] the group is protected[17] and there is intent to destroy, indicated through the Muggle-born Registration Commission. As international criminal law is targeted at the crimes of individuals, it will be up to a wizarding court to hold trial against those leading the Muggle-born Registration Commission, which would as a start certainly be Dolores Umbridge, Corban Yaxley, Albert Runcorn, Travers, John Dawlish and Mafalda Hopkirk.[18] For further death eaters to accuse of genocide we'd have to assess their specific acts but there is certainly room for further exploration.

5.3 Are the Death Eaters Committing Crimes Against Humanity?

5.3.1 What Are Crimes Against Humanity?

Art. 7 Rome Statute

1. For the purpose of this Statute, "crimes against humanity" means any of the following acts when committed as part of a widespread or systematic attack directed against any civilian population, with knowledge of the attack:
   (a) Murder;
   (b) Extermination;
   (c) Enslavement;
   (d) Deportation or forcible transfer of population;

---

[16] As required based on Art. 6 Rome Statue and discussed in Sect. 5.2.1.

[17] Muggle-borns and half-blood witches and wizards will be seen as a protected group under Art. 6 Rome Statue, as discussed in Sect. 5.2.2.2.

[18] More in Harry Potter Fandom (n.d.).

(e) Imprisonment or other severe deprivation of physical liberty in violation of fundamental rules of international law;

(f) Torture;

(g) Rape, sexual slavery, enforced prostitution, forced pregnancy, enforced sterilization, or any other form of sexual violence of comparable gravity;

(h) Persecution against any identifiable group or collectivity on political, racial, national, ethnic, cultural, religious, gender as defined in paragraph 3, or other grounds that are universally recognized as impermissible under international law, in connection with any act referred to in this paragraph or any crime within the jurisdiction of the Court;

(i) Enforced disappearance of persons;

(j) The crime of apartheid;

(k) Other inhumane acts of a similar character intentionally causing great suffering, or serious injury to body or to mental or physical health.

The most important aspect about crimes against humanity is that the criminal acts are committed systematically by a state or an organized group, linked to an agreed plan. Those who commit the crimes have to know about this overall plan.[19] The crimes do not have to be linked to an armed conflict, but can occur at any point.[20]

The majority of these crimes are easy enough to understand, such as murder, enslavement, torture or rape.[21] The one crime that is relevant to our case and requires a bit more discussion is persecution against any identifiable group or collectivity. Unlike with genocide, it refers to a broader range of groups here. This includes "political, racial, national, ethnic, cultural, religious, gender or other grounds".[22] Here we don't need the intention to fully eliminate the group, but pure persecution suffices.

5.3.2   Would the Acts of the Death Eaters Fall Under the Definition of Crimes Against Humanity?

Again, the period that will be most relevant to assess links to potential crimes against humanity is after the Battle in the Ministry of Magic when the death eaters moved out into the open. Before then, the death eaters were primarily gathering their strength and were not active as openly, therefore also not following an overall plan that would be sufficiently visible to us as neutral observers. We will not focus

---

[19]For more details on this: https://www.un.org/en/genocideprevention/crimes-against-humanity.shtml.

[20]For a deeper insight into crimes against humanity, refer to: Cassese and Gaeta (2013), pp. 84 ff.; Bassiouni (1999).

[21]For more details on what each of these entail please look into Cassese and Gaeta (2013), pp. 84 ff.

[22]Art. 7 (1) h Rome Statute.

on individual death eaters in this section, but this will need to be done once a wizarding court takes up the task of assessing crimes against humanity.

5.3.2.1 Do the Acts of the Death Eaters Fall Under the List of Specific Attacks?

There are a couple of acts that can qualify as crimes listed under Art. 7 Rome Statute. Those include the use of the *Cruciatus* Curse by multiple death eaters during their fights (just think of Bellatrix Lestrange using the curse on Hermione in Malfoy Manor), the killing of Muggles (remember the attack on the Brockdale and Millennium Bridge) as well as Muggle-borns (beyond Azkaban, there were also several killings of Muggle-borns by death eaters), imprisonment of Muggle-borns and persecution of Muggles as well as Muggle-borns and halfbloods.

Most of these are very straight forward but let us take a closer look at persecution. As discussed earlier, Muggle-borns and halfbloods can qualify as protected groups also linked to the stricter norm on genocide.[23] The same is certainly true for Muggles when following the broader definition of persecution. But what acts are considered persecution?

As highlighted in Art. 7 (2) Rome Statute, persecution is the "intentional and severe deprivation of fundamental rights contrary to international law by reason of the identity of the group or collectivity". Essentially, this means that because you are member of a certain group (e.g., a Muggle or Muggle-born) someone is denying you your basic rights (e.g. freedom or property). Sounds familiar? Yes indeed, another clear case for the death eaters. They are certainly persecuting Muggles, Muggle-borns and half-blood witches and wizards purely because they belong to this group. The act therefore also falls under Art. 7 (2) h.

5.3.2.2 Are the Acts Part of a Widespread or Systematic Attack Against the Civilian Population?

The first question is whether the attacks are conducted against the civilian population. For the overwhelming majority of cases, the answer is yes. There are some cases, in which attacks might be conducted against civilians directly participating in hostilities (think about the members of the Order of the Phoenix during the Battle of Hogwarts), but many of the victims were either completely clueless civilians (the Muggles on the bridge) or members of the civilian population who were not engaged in the fighting (the many Muggle-borns sent to Azkaban).

The other question is whether there was a widespread or systematic attack. Again, this is relatively easy to answer. Given Voldemort's continuous trust issues, he never really trusted anyone to run operations independently. This also means, that everything that happened was at least to some degree part of his larger plan to reestablish supremacy in the wizarding world and get rid of unwanted groups. While his followers might not have known every aspect of this plan, they were certainly aware of the plan's existence and the overall ambition. The acts were therefore

---

[23] See above Sect. 5.2.

part of a widespread and systematic attack. This means that even the last element of crimes against humanity is given.

So yes, all in all, the death eaters committed crimes against humanity. What a development for a series that started as children's books about a boy, a school and magic.

5.4 Completing the List: Are the Death Eaters Committing War Crimes?

5.4.1 Looking at the Definition of War Crimes

As you will be able to see from the long box below, Art. 8 Rome Statute is quite something. There are a couple of dimensions to this crime. First, we have to differentiate between the parts of Art. 8 linked to IAC and those linked to NIAC.

Yes, there are different rules in IAC and NIAC. This is lovingly called the "two box approach" because, you guessed it, we are assessing these situations as if they were in two separate boxes.[24]

Art. 8 Rome Statute

1. The court shall have jurisdiction in respect of war crimes in particular when committed as part of a plan or policy or as part of a large-scale commission of such crimes.
2. For the purpose of this Statute, "war crimes" means:
   (a) Grave breaches of the Geneva Conventions of 12 August 1949, namely, any of the following acts against persons or property protected under the provisions of the relevant Geneva Convention:
      i. Wilful killing;
      ii. Torture or inhuman treatment, including biological experiments;
      iii. Wilfully causing great suffering, or serious injury to body or health;
      iv. Extensive destruction and appropriation of property, not justified by military necessity and carried out unlawfully and wantonly;
      (...)
   (b) Other serious violations of the laws and customs applicable in international armed conflict, within the established framework of international law, namely, any of the following acts:
      i. Intentionally directing attacks against the civilian population as such or against individual civilians not taking direct part in hostilities;
      ii. Intentionally directing attacks against civilian objects, that is, objects which are not military objectives;
      (...)

---

[24] If this approach intrigues you, more details can be found here: Akande (2012), pp. 32 ff.; Sager (2011), pp. 36 ff.

(c) In the case of an armed conflict not of an international character, serious violations of article 3 common to the four Geneva Conventions of 12 August 1949, namely, any of the following acts committed against persons taking no active part in hostilities, including members of armed forces who laid down their arms and those placed *hors de combat* by sickness, wounds, detention or any other cause:
   i. Violence to life and person, in particular murder of all kinds, mutilation, cruel treatment and torture;
   ii. Committing outrages upon personal dignity, in particular humiliating and degrading treatment;
      (...)
(d) Paragraph 2 (c) applies to armed conflicts not of an international character and thus does not apply to situations of internal disturbances and tensions, such as riots, isolated and sporadic acts of violence, or other acts of a similar nature.
(e) Other serious violations of the laws and customs applicable in armed conflicts not of an international character, within the framework of international law, namely, any of the following acts:
   i. Intentionally directing attacks against the civilian population as such or against individual civilians not taking direct part in hostilities;
      (...)

But before going deeper into these two boxes, it is important for you to understand that war crimes—as the name kind of suggests—only exist linked to an ongoing conflict. There are no war crimes during peace. In those situations, it would be crimes against humanity we have to look at. There needs to be a link between the crime committed and the ongoing armed conflict (the so-called *nexus*).[25] This is also quite straightforward. Imagine there is an armed conflict going on in your country. Your neighbor is a distant relative of Lucius Malfoy. This neighbor has always been fighting with the other people living on your street. One day, he gets up and blows up the house of one of these neighbors. Luckily, no one dies but the property is completely destroyed. Would this be a war crime? Well, there is an armed conflict and there is the extensive destruction of property. But it does not have any link to the armed conflict. So no, it is not a war crime but an ordinary criminal act. Still illegal, needs to be punished, but not under international criminal law. The last two elements needed for a war crime are a serious violation of international humanitarian law that is listed under the war crimes for Art. 8 Rome Statute and the fulfillment of all objective and subjective elements of the crime (meaning you have done all preparations that are required for the relevant crime and you were intending to do it).

War crimes cover both violations of the "Law of Geneva" and the "Law of the Hague". "Law of Geneva" refers to the treaties dealing with the protection of victims

---

[25] Kälin and Künzli (2010), p. 62.

of armed conflicts, as codified in the Geneva Conventions of 1949.[26] "Law of the Hague" refers to the rules dealing with the conduct of hostilities, establishing limitations or prohibitions of means and methods of warfare based on the Hague Conventions of 1899 and 1907.[27]

Now back to our two boxes. Why are there different rules during IAC and NIAC, you might wonder. Well, we kind of have to appreciate that there are war crimes during NIAC to begin with. Initially, war crimes were only linked to IAC. In the Tadić decision the ICTY expanded war crimes also to NIAC, which was then also copied in the Statute of the ICTR.[28] The Rome Statute now includes both war crimes during IAC and NIAC.

There are, however, still some discrepancies between what is forbidden in an IAC and a NIAC. If you don't believe me, read through the entire Art. 8 Rome Statute and count how many crimes are forbidden in each type of conflict.

When looking at war crimes during IAC, Art. 8 (2) (a) focuses on grave breaches of GC I-IV and Art. 8 (2) (b) focuses on serious violations of the laws and customs in IAC, taken mainly from the 1907 Hague Convention respecting the Laws and Customs of War on Land, AP I, the 1899 Hague Declaration Concerning Expanding Bullets and the 1925 Geneva Gas Protocol.[29]

Linked to war crimes during NIAC, Art. 8 (2) (c) focuses on serious violations of common Art. 3 GC I-IV and Art. 8 (2) (d) focuses on serious violations of AP II and the 1907 Hague Regulations.[30]

5.4.2 Do the Acts of the Death Eaters Constitute War Crimes?

First, we have to understand what acts of the death eaters we want to consider. For this, let us briefly recap the requirements for war crimes:

1) Ongoing armed conflict
2) Nexus between the crime committed and the ongoing armed conflict
3) Crime is listed in Art. 8 Rome Statute for the relevant type of conflict
4) All objective and subjective elements of the crime fulfilled

The first question will therefore be if we have an ongoing armed conflict. As discussed earlier, there is a NIAC during the Battle of Hogwarts, when death eaters

---

[26]ICRC (n.d.-a).

[27]ICRC (n.d.-b).

[28]ICTY, *Prosecutor v. Dusko Tadić a/k/a 'Dule'*, IT-94-1, Appeals Chamber, Decision on the Defense Motion for Interlocutory Appeal on Jurisdiction, 2 October 1995, §119. The ICTR Statute reflected this in Art. 4.

[29]Dörmann (2003), pp. 343–344.

[30]Dörmann (2003), pp. 344–345.

fight against the Order of the Phoenix, loyal Hogwarts professors and a group of volunteers.[31]

The core question is whether the death eaters committed any of the relevant crimes (Art. 8 (2) (c)–(e)) with a link to the armed conflict during this battle. Let us take a look at the possible crimes and see which ones seem most relevant. One potential war crime that immediately comes to mind is violence to life and person (Art. 8 (2) (c) (i)), in particular murder and torture. Yet, is this really the case? Let's recap—there only is an ongoing armed conflict during the Battle at Hogwarts. So while the initial instant might be to scream "Yes, this is all given" let us pause for a moment. Art. 8 (2) (c) is limited to attacks "committed against persons taking no active part in hostilities, including members of armed forces who laid down their arms and those placed hors de combat by sickness, wounds, detention". It will therefore be essential to establish whether the death eaters attacked anyone who was either not a civilian directly participating in hostilities or *hors de combat*.

Our first question to consider is therefore whether the death eaters were fighting against anyone not taking active part in hostilities. In general yes, but during the critical phase of the Battle of Hogwarts there is limited evidence that they did. The other question is therefore whether they were committing attacks against anyone who was considered *hors de combat*. This can only link to those sick or wounded as the death eaters were not detaining anyone during the battle. Yes, there were many wounded, especially in the second half of the battle, after Harry had gone to seek Voldemort in the Forbidden Forest and had—allegedly—been killed. Yet, even though the death eaters were fighting against witches and wizards who had been previously injured, they all entered the fight voluntarily. It was not as if the death eaters attacked the Great Hall even though everyone inside had given up. The death eaters did therefore not commit war crimes, as the civilians were all still directly participating in hostilities and in an active fight against them.

5.5   Could Voldemort Be Held Accountable for Leading the Death Eaters?

Voldemort has certainly committed numerous crimes by himself. Just think of the many people he killed, whether Muggles, goblins or witches and wizards. But there is even more to it. There are also the numerous crimes that the death eaters committed on his behalf or following his direct orders. Let us take a look at how we might be able to also hold him accountable for these crimes. There are two key options that will be relevant to look at: command responsibility and the construct of a joint criminal enterprise (JCE).

---

[31] If you want to read up on why we argued this, please go back here: Sect. 3.2.1.

5.5.1   Command Responsibility as Option to Hold Voldemort Accountable

Command responsibility means that a superior (which can be in a military or a civilian hierarchy) can be held criminally responsible for international crimes his subordinates commit. This rule has found its way into the Rome Statute in Art. 28.

Art. 28 Rome Statute

In addition to other grounds of criminal responsibility under this Statute for crimes within the jurisdiction of the Court:

(a) A military commander or person effectively acting as a military commander shall be criminally responsible for crimes within the jurisdiction of the Court committed by forces under his or her effective command and control, or effective authority and control as the case may be, as a result of his or her failure to exercise control properly over such forces, where:
   i. That military commander or person either knew or, owing to the circumstances at the time, should have known that the forces were committed or about to commit such crimes; and
   ii. That the military commander or person failed to take all necessary and reasonable measures within his or her power to prevent or repress their commission or to submit the matter to the competent authorities for investigation and prosecution.

(...)

Superior responsibility is linked to failure to prevent or repress, making it a crime of omission. For superior responsibility to be given we need the following three elements: (1) the effective command and control; (2) a commander who "knew or should have known" of the crimes; and (3) the failure to take the reasonable and necessary measures.[32]

When applying command responsibility to the death eaters' crimes and Voldemort's role we have to assess whether Voldemort was either the military commander or the person effectively acting as a military commander who knew or should have known of the crimes and did not take any reasonable or necessary measures to prevent them.[33]

---

[32] More on this in: van der Wilt (2017).

[33] Many commanders were found guilty based on this logic, starting with those during World War II (both Germans as well as Japanese commanders). More on this, including links to relevant cases such as the Yamashita case: Henckaerts and Doswald-Beck (2005), p. 559.

In this case, it is rather straightforward. Voldemort was clearly in command. While the death eaters are not an official military structure, he de facto acted as a military commander for them. They were reporting to him (just think back of him residing in Malfoy Manor),[34] he was giving them orders on what to do and whom to target, they were returning those they had captured to him. There is also no doubt that Voldemort was fully aware of the genocide that was committed in his name as well as the crimes against humanity, many of which he committed himself. He also clearly did not take any reasonable or necessary measures to stop the death eaters from continuing with their atrocities. Instead, he was an active part in their criminal activities and in the majority of cases the mastermind behind the attacks.

The relevant requirements for command responsibility are therefore given and Voldemort could be held responsible.

5.5.2 The Death Eaters as a Joint Criminal Enterprise

The other alternative is the concept of a JCE. Before any of you aspiring lawyers shout out—yes, I know that the ICC is not using the JCE doctrine anymore.[35] But other tribunals did. And as we don't know which theories hypothetical wizarding tribunals will follow, let us at least take a look at the different options there are. As part of the JCE doctrine, members of a group can be held accountable for the acts of the group if they are driven by a common plan or purpose.

The JCE doctrine was developed in the Tadic trial of 1999 by the ICTY.[36] The ICTY identified three categories of JCE. The first one is considered the "basic form" and it concerns cases in which all co-perpetrators have a common purpose and the same criminal intention. The second form is the "systemic form" that is characterized by an organized system of ill-treatment, as for example given in concentration camps, in which prisoners are systematically mistreated or killed. The third category is the "extended" form that covers cases with a common purpose to commit a crime, in which one of the perpetrators commits an act that is outside the common purpose, but still considered a natural and foreseeable consequence deriving from this common purpose.[37]

The requirements for JCE are that the accused person must have acted with a number of other persons. They do not have to be part of a military, political or administrative structure. Yet, they need to at least act with a common plan or purpose, which does, however, not need to be previously arranged or formulated. Essentially this means that you don't need a membership charter that specifically states what your criminal plan is, but there needs to be a plan.

---

[34] If you cannot immediately recall, read up on this here: Rowling (2007), Chapter 1: The Dark Lord Ascending.

[35] If you want to read up on it, please go here: Minkova (2022), pp. 510–538.

[36] ICTY, Prosecutor v. Tadić (IT-94-1), Appeals Chamber, Judgment (15 July 1999).

[37] More on this in: Ambos (2007), pp. 159–183.

There is no specific requirement linked to the type of participation. These are the objective requirements (everything we can see and observe). There are also several subjective requirements (linked to what the perpetrator must have thought).[38] These are different depending on the type of JCE. If we consider the basic form, we only need the shared intent of all co-perpetrators to commit a certain crime. For the systemic form we also need knowledge of the system of ill-treatment and intent to further this system. For the extended form, responsibility for crimes that go beyond the original plan arises "only if, under the circumstances of the case, (i) it was foreseeable that such a crime might be perpetrated by one or other members of the group and (ii) the accused willingly took that risk".[39]

Let us be honest—this is quite a straightforward one. But for the sake of practice let me go step by step. Yes, the death eaters were acting with a number of others (I hereby challenge you to list as many death eaters names as you can remember). They had a common plan and purpose, basically linked to their overall pure-blood ideology and of course anything that Voldemort was telling them to do (including through their common low-tech communication arm tattoo). Now on to the subjective requirements. The shared intent to commit the impressive (in a negative way of course) list of crimes was certainly given. The death eaters knew that their group was no scout club—the beforementioned mark on their arm kind of already says it all. The basic form of JCE is therefore certainly given—definitely in the time post Voldemort's return but to some degree, and for some group members, also before that (think about Quirrel's attack on Harry and Lucius Malfoy sneaking the diary into Hogwarts as examples of sustained group activity). For the systemic form we'd need knowledge of the system of ill-treatment and intent to further this system. Let's just take the case of their treatment of Muggle-borns and sending them to Azkaban. The death eaters will have known of this and were furthering it by hunting them down and bringing them to the Muggle-born Registration Commission. So even the systemic form of JCE will be given for many death eaters. But what about the extended form? Well, how foreseeable is it that a group of Muggle-born hating witches and wizards commits crimes that might go beyond their direct mission statement? I'm not even going to debate this. Even the extended form of responsibility can be accepted for the death eaters and their leader.

---

[38] More in Ambos (2007), pp. 160–161.

[39] Tadić Appeal Judgment, para 228. For more on the differences between JCE and command responsibility as well as the depth of case law on this, I'll ask you to check out this article (and yes, there is even a link included, life is good): Ambos (2007), pp. 159–183, https://www.legal-tools. org/doc/369c3e/pdf/.

5.6   Can We Bring the Death Eaters or Even Voldemort to the Hague?

When looking at ways to ensure responsibility for international crimes, we will focus our assessment on the ICC. Not just because this makes our life easier but also as it makes sense. There is no special tribunal linked to the activities of the death eaters, at least not that we know of. The sole option in the international arena is the ICC.

As mentioned earlier, the ICC has jurisdiction for the most serious crimes of international concern, including genocide, war crimes and crimes against humanity. These are certainly given, as we just discussed. The next relevant question is whether jurisdiction *ratione temporis* was given. In case you have forgotten what this means, no worries. It means whether the relevant statute (in this case the Rome Statute) was in force and whether the relevant state had ratified it at the time of the alleged offense.

In this case, we don't need to go deep into questions about whether Britain could be seen as the relevant state given that some of the crimes were committed on British territory and against Muggles. As the Battle of Hogwarts—based on information available to us—occurred in May 1998[40] the crimes precede the UK's ratification of the Rome Statute, which only occurred in 2001.[41]

So no, neither the death eaters nor Voldemort can be brought to the Hague. Yet, this might also be ok. Bear with me. At least some of the culprits reportedly had to stand trial for their actions, as did for example Dolores Umbridge.[42] Many other death eaters had fallen during the Battle at Hogwarts, as did Bellatrix Lestrange. Yes, some will have gotten away (just think Lucius Malfoy), but there at least was an attempt to restore justice from within the wizarding community itself. I would love to provide you with more details about these trials and the crimes that the perpetrators were convinced for but unfortunately there is a lack of reliable evidence for these trials.

References

Akande D (2012) Classification of armed conflicts: relevant legal concepts. In: Wilmshurst E (ed) International law and the classification of conflicts. Oxford University Press, Oxford, pp 32–79

Ambos K (2007) Joint criminal enterprise and command responsibility. J Int Crim Just 5:159–183

Bassiouni M (1999) Crimes against humanity in international criminal law, 2nd edn. Kluwer Law International, The Hague

Cassese A, Gaeta P (2013) Cassese's international criminal law, 3rd edn. Oxford University Press, Oxford

---

[40] Rowling (2015a).

[41] If you want to fact check this, go here: https://asp.icc-cpi.int/states-parties/western-european-and-other-states/united-kingdom.

[42] Rowling (2015a).

Dörmann K (2003) War crimes under the Rome Statute of the International Criminal Court, with a special focus on the negotiations of the elements of crimes. In: von Bogdandy A, Wolfrum R (eds) Max Planck Yearbook of United Nations Law. Martinus Nijhoff, Leiden, pp 341–407

Harry Potter Fandom (n.d.) Muggle-Born Registration Commission. https://harrypotter.fandom.com/wiki/Muggle-Born_Registration_Commission. Accessed 20 Dec 2022

Henckaerts J-M, Doswald-Beck L (eds) (2005) Customary international humanitarian law: Volume I: Rules. Cambridge University Press, Cambridge

ICRC (n.d.-a) Law of Geneva. https://casebook.icrc.org/glossary/law-geneva. Accessed 20 Dec 2022

ICRC (n.d.-b) Law of the Hague. https://casebook.icrc.org/glossary/law-hague. Accessed 20 Dec 2022

Kälin W, Künzli J (2010) The law of international human rights protection. Oxford University Press, Oxford

Lingaas C (2015) Defining the protected groups of genocide through the case law of international courts. ICD Brief 18. https://www.internationalcrimesdatabase.org/upload/documents/20151217T122733-Lingaas%20Final%20ICD%20Format.pdf. Accessed 20 Dec 2022

Maison R (2010) Le crime de génocide dans la jurisprudence internationale: débats et hypothèses. In: Tomuschat C, Lagrange E, Oeter S (eds) The right to life. Martinus Nijhoff, Leiden, pp 95–119

Minkova LG (2022) Control over the theory: reforming the ICC's approach to establishing commission liability? Int Crim Law Rev 22:510–538

Rowling JK (2003) Harry Potter and the order of the phoenix. Bloomsbury, London

Rowling JK (2007) Harry Potter and the deathly hallows. Bloomsbury, London

Rowling JK (2015a) Dolores Umbridge. https://www.wizardingworld.com/writing-by-jk-rowling/dolores-umbridge. Accessed 20 Dec 2022

Rowling JK (2015b) Pure-blood. https://www.wizardingworld.com/writing-by-jk-rowling/pure-blood. Accessed 20 Dec 2022

Sager C (2011) Voraussetzungen der Strafbarkeit von Kriegsverbrechen im nicht-internationalen bewaffneten Konflikt: Bringt Rom, was Genf braucht? Helbing Lichtenhahn, Basel

Schabas W (2009) Genocide in international law, 2nd edn. Cambridge University Press, Cambridge

Shaw MN (2017) International law, 8th edn. Cambridge University Press, Cambridge

van der Wilt H (2017) Command responsibility. Oxford Bibliographies. https://www.oxfordbibliographies.com/view/document/obo-9780199796953/obo-9780199796953-0088.xml. Accessed 20 Dec 2022

Werle G, Jeßberger F (2020) Principles of international criminal law, 4th edn. Oxford University Press, Oxford

Air Law

6

Abstract

With the big questions around criminal accountability answered, let us look at the more pragmatic concerns in the wizarding world. Particularly, let us look at the skies. The question we aim to answer is how air travel is regulated—especially given all the different options such as flying brooms, using carpets or just pure levitation (and of course the likes of Voldemort who can fly without broom). And can broomsticks be seen as the equivalent of a fighter jet, given that wizards on brooms can be armed with their wand and wreak havoc from the skies?

6.1 Why Are We Talking About Air Law Now?

This might feel like a stretch. But trust me, air law is highly fascinating and more relevant than you might think. Without it, readers like yourself would not be able to fly out of your own country and visit any of these exciting destinations you might have been dreaming about. Why, you might ask yourself? Well, because you cannot simply land an airplane wherever you want if you are an official airline. You need permission to do so. And these permissions need to be granted by sovereign states. But let us look more closely at what we understand as air law to give you deeper insights into this topic.

6.2 Is There a Wizarding Version of Air Law?

6.2.1 How Is Air Travel Regulated?

Air law links to the fundamental principle of sovereignty of one's territory. It's a bit like if you own your own house (and no, I'm unfortunately not speaking of experience, thanks inflation and housing bubble): you don't want anyone to trespass, that is obvious. But you'll certainly also not want anyone landing their helicopter on your imaginary backyard. For governments, the sky above their territory is like an extension of their sovereign territory. Which is why, quite naturally, we have laws regulating what is allowed in this airspace.[1]

Air law is a relatively new branch of international law compared to IHL. Why is that you might ask. Well, simply because we humans figured out how to violently kill each other before we figured out how to fly. Hence, IHL was there before air law. Initial attempts at regulating what goes on in the skies started early in the last century.[2]

There are many different aspects to air law. They range from sovereignty of national airspace to dispute settlement in international civil aviation (remember, most people need to buy plane tickets to travel far and there can always be issues resulting from that, if there is a delay or overbooking) and other issues such as safety standards and liability.[3] Here, we will only focus on sovereignty in airspace.

So, what does sovereignty in airspace mean? Regulation on this can be found in the Chicago Convention on International Civil Aviation 1944.[4] The Chicago Convention focuses on civil aviation only, as opposed to state aircraft. If you wonder what this means, well as the name says. One is linked to state activity, which can be military, custom or police activity. The other is linked to economic activity, meaning the transport of people or goods over the territory. Obviously, the more problematic aspect is state activity, when we consider it from a perspective of state sovereignty.

6.2.1.1 Regulation of Civil Aviation

Let us start with the simple regulation first—civil aviation. As we understood, there is state sovereignty over airspace. That means an aircraft from another country cannot just enter this airspace. All of this is laid down in Art. 1 and 2 of the Chicago Convention.

Art. 1 Chicago Convention

The contracting States recognize that every State has complete and exclusive sovereignty over the airspace above its territory.

Art. 2 Chicago Convention

---

[1] More on the basics of air law in this research guide: https://peacepalacelibrary.nl/research-guide/air-law.

[2] On this you can find more details in: Shaw (2017), pp. 403–404.

[3] If you want to learn more about all these others topics, check out: de Leon (2022). There are also many fascinating regulations linked to compensation you can receive for flight delays or lost/damaged baggage. As this seems less relevant to wizards and witches, we will skip these questions here.

[4] Chicago Convention on International Civil Aviation, 7 December 1944, 15 UNTS 295.

For the purpose of this Convention the territory of a State shall be deemed to be the land areas and territorial waters adjacent thereto under the sovereignty, suzerainty, protection of mandate of such State.

But that would be kind of a bummer when we think about anything from travel to logistics. And it does not really reflect the reality we see on the ground. Therefore, we have found a solution for this problem. The solution is mentioned in Art. 6 Chicago Convention and it is called Air Service Agreement (ASA). These ASAs manage the right of aircraft to land. They are typically concluded between two states (therefore called bilateral agreements). There are currently over 4000 bilateral ASAs.[5]

These ASAs don't always grant the same types of rights. There is a list of freedoms that can be granted as part of ASAs. The first five freedoms are officially recognized freedoms based on international treaties. The others are therefore only "so-called" freedoms. Let's take a look at these freedoms one by one:[6]

- First Freedom: fly across the territory without landing (imagine the carriage of Beauxbatons flying over the Netherlands on the way to Hogwarts)
- Second Freedom: land in the territory for non-traffic purposes (on the way, the horses get thirsty and require a stop for some single-malt whiskey—unfortunately in Belgium, which is not the prime single-malt location)
- Third Freedom: put down traffic coming from the home state of the carrier in the other state (Beauxbatons students exit the carriage in Hogwarts)
- Fourth Freedom: take on traffic destined for the home state of the carrier in the other state (Beauxbatons students enter the carriage to return to their school)
- Fifth Freedom: put down and take on traffic coming from or destined to a third state (the carriage stops over in Germany and two exchange students get off the carriage before the flight continues to France)
- Sixth Freedom: transport traffic moving between two others states via the home state of the carrier (the carriage starts in Hogwarts, lands in France and then continues on to the coast of Spain)
- Seventh Freedom: transport traffic between territory of granting state and any third state (the carriage flies directly from Hogwarts to Spain without a stop in France)

---

[5]If you want to see what the template for such an ASA looks like, visit this website: https://www. icao.int/sustainability/pages/eap_ep_tasa.aspx. Each country's ministry of transportation (might be called differently, but the ministry in charge of air traffic, among others) has the list of the bilateral ASAs that this country has signed. For an example of such an ASA, here the one between the Philippine and the United States: https://www.officialgazette.gov.ph/1946/12/01/air-transport-agreement-between-the-united-states-of-america-and-the-republic-of-the-philippines/. For a data-base of all ASAs: https://www.icao.int/sustainability/pages/Doc9511.aspx.

[6]To reassure you that the weird wording was not my idea: https://www.icao.int/pages/freedomsair. aspx.

– Eighth Freedom: transport cabotage traffic (cabotage means you transport people or goods within two points in the same country) between two points in territory of granting state on service which starts or ends in home country of the foreign carrier or outside the territory of the granting state (the carriage makes two stops in Scotland to collect some of the best single-malt whiskey, before returning to France)
– Ninth Freedom: transport cabotage traffic entirely within territory of another state (the carriage flies between two locations in Scotland, the horses get too drunk to continue on—it is a purely domestic flight in Scotland)

Ok, granted, this is a lot. The key aspect that you have to take away from this—if you want to land, pick up people/cargo or bring people/cargo to a location in a different country, you better make sure that the state in which your airline is registered has signed an ASA with the other government. And of course, not every airline will then be allowed to fly to the other country, there are limitations.

6.2.1.2 Regulation of State Aviation and in Particular Military Overflight
Now that we have a broad understanding of how civil aviation works, what about military overflight or any other type of state activity in the airspace of another country? Art. 3 Chicago Convention helps us out—essentially, the same rules apply for state aircraft. If you want to fly over another state's territory, you have to ask for permission.[7]

Art. 3 Chicago Convention

a) This Convention shall be applicable only to civil aircraft, and shall not be applicable to state aircraft.
b) Aircraft used in military, customs and police services shall be deemed to be state aircraft.
c) No state aircraft of a contracting State shall fly over the territory of another State or land thereon without authorization by special agreement or otherwise, and in accordance with the terms thereof.

But it is not as straightforward as it sounds. One particular cause for discussion in the past couple of years were the so-called Air Defense Identification Zones (ADIZ). To take the suspense away right from the start—ADIZ are not an international law instrument, they are completely bogus and a political tool that several governments use. Not more, not less. Try searching for them in international treaties, you will not

[7]This, of course, does not always work out as planned. One example of a state asking for permission—but not really—was when in 2022 the U.S. Air Force requested permission to fly a KC-10 tanker across Austrian airspace and forgot to mention that it would be accompanied by two F-117 stealth fighters. The permission was only granted for the tanker and it caused significant diplomatic uproar and public outcry. More on this in: Karnitschnig (2003). More on the rules linked to state aviation and military aircraft: Bourbonniere and Haeck (2001).

find them. But as several governments continue to claim an absurd right to regulate airspace that is beyond their territorial waters, let me give you the gist of what this is about, so that you are well informed, have the facts at hand and can then happily go on ignoring these claims in the future.

An ADIZ is essentially a unilaterally established zone in international air space.[8] Yes, this should tip you off already—unilateral and international air space. Essentially, an ADIZ creates an obligation for civil or military aircraft to report a flight plan before entering a country's territory. This is all fun and games, it might even have benefits for national security and geopolitics if everyone has some peace of mind, yet the question of where you apply this rule matters greatly. If only over national territory, in the air above that is legitimately considered a states airspace, this is ok. A lot of countries do it, including the U.S. (as in many cases, the first one to start this trend, back in 1950), but also a couple of South Asian countries (Pakistan, India, Bangladesh), some European countries (e.g., U.K, Norway) and several nations across East Asia (China, Taiwan, North Korea, South Korea) to just name a few.[9] Now why all the fuzz? Well, many countries don't just stick to the airspace above their territory but get a bit more creative in defining what falls within their ADIZ. Many—for reasons that are not linked in international law but more in convenience as adding another abbreviations just sounds smart and might confuse one or the other—link their ADIZ to their Exclusive Economic Zone (EEZ). We will talk about the EEZ in the next chapter when we tackle law of the sea. Important for you to remember is that the EEZ is a zone that expands beyond the territorial waters and grants certain rights linked to maritime resources. Maritime resources, not airspace. As the International Civil Aviation Organization brilliantly describes (including a great visual, look it up), sovereign national airspace extends of the landmass of a state and its territorial waters.[10] That's it.

6.2.2   What Are the Types of Air Travel in the Wizarding World?

Now on to the core question: how is air travel regulated in the wizarding world or how should it be regulated? Let us start by understanding how air travel works for witches and wizards. Witches and wizards are not able to fly unaided in human form. Well, aside from Voldemort in his final stage. But otherwise usually not. So let us look at how they fly or travel to then be able to discuss regulation of these means of transportation.

---

[8]Bourbonniere and Haeck (2001), p. 953.

[9]More on this in: Bakhtiar et al. (2016), p. 17.

[10]Look it up, this is the brilliant visual providing more detailed insights into where the boundaries are: https://www.icao.int/APAC/Documents/edocs/International%20Airspace%20and %20Civil-Military%20Cooperation.pdf. If you want to read up on more details about ADIZ, check out Bakhtiar et al. (2016).

There are reports of a few Animagi who are able to transform into winged creatures and can fly. Yet, there are challenges to overcome. If one for example transforms into a bat, one can fly but given that one now has a bat's brain, it is unlikely that one will remember where to fly.[11] Travel into other wizarding countries as bat or other "regular" flying animal (excluding dragons that would slightly disturb Muggles) would not be an issue concerning air law.

Levitation is another ability to lift up, yet hovering a few feet above the ground just does not come close to actually flying. And it really does not lead to any questions about sovereignty of air space, unless a group of witches and wizards suddenly decides to hold a levitation flashmob at the border between two wizarding states. And if that happens, let us be honest, it would be worth it.

In the Middle East, the common means of wizarding transport is a carpet. In the UK carpets are listed in the Registry of Proscribed Charmable Objects and defined as Muggle artifacts illegal to enchant. Moreover, there is the option to travel by bewitched objects such as flying cars. But we don't even need to discuss the legality of travelling between wizarding countries in a flying car as the fact that the car is able to fly is an offense in itself[12], at least in the UK.

In the West, witches and wizards chose to bewitch an object they could easily hide from Muggles. The broomstick was the ideal object given that its presence in the home was easy to explain, it is easily portable and inexpensive—unless you want to go for the fastest and newest one that Broomstix has to offer.[13]

Another type of travel, though not strictly speaking really via air, is the Floo Network, an important link between wizarding locations. One of the advantages of the Floo Network is that it is not breaking the International Statute of Secrecy as when using broomsticks and there is no danger of serious injury or splinching as when relying on Apparition (we get there in a minute). Moreover, the Floo Network can be used to transport children. The Ministry of Magic needs to issue a permission for a fireplace to become connected to the Floo Network (the underlying logic of the Floo Network is then a bit like beaming between two places). Muggle fireplaces can only be joined up in cases of emergency and on a temporary basis. But while fascinating, there is limited relevance to discuss air travel.

Apparition is another magical method of travel. Wizards have to be of age to apparate and they have to take an Apparition test. Apparating without license is illegal. This rule is enforced by the Department of Magical Transportation. It can best be equated to the driving test. If the wizards don't properly focus on the three Ds (Destination, Determination, Deliberation), they might end up splinching, meaning they have body parts in two places at once. Underage wizards and wizards without apparition license can still benefit from this mode of transportation through side-along apparition with an adult. There is a range limit to apparition and even wizards

---

[11] Whisp (n.d.), p. 3.

[12] Rowling (1998), Chapter 6: Gilderoy Lockhart.

[13] More details on the journey from broomsticks used in AD 962 to the Nimbus 2000 can be found in: Whisp (n.d.), pp. 5–6; 89, 92.

such as Voldemort don't attempt to apparate beyond Britain (as shown when he visited Nurmengard).[14] Given that there is no apparition between countries, there is also less of a need to focus on this in more detail when discussing air travel between countries.

Portkeys are enchanted objects which allow wizards to travel to pre-specified locations. Through the use of the *Portus* spell, objects are transformed into portkeys. Their creation is regulated by the Portkey Office of the Department of Magical Transportation. During the 1994 Quidditch World Cup, timed portkeys were used to transport witches and wizards wanted to watch the tournament. Some witches and wizards rely on illegal portkeys to travel internationally (as Newt Scamander and Jacob Kowalski did to travel from Dover to France). So yes, portkeys seem to be worth watching out for when it comes to regulating international travel. While they are not per se flying objects that can be seen, they transport people via air from one place to another—imagine an aircraft that is so fast you cannot see it—likely the closest you can get to what a portkey does.

6.2.3   What Type of Regulation Could Be Applied to the Wizarding World?

As we established before, the most relevant forms of witches and wizards air travel for the purpose of this book and focusing on Britain are by broomstick or portkey. So, are there any ASAs between wizarding nations that would regulate this type of air travel? And what if witches and wizards end up fighting while on a broom, does it mean that the broom is the wizarding equivalent of a fighter jet? Well, let us find out.

Let us start with portkeys as they are more straightforward. There is a purely civilian application for transport with a portkey (before you want to protest, please tell me how anyone would be hurting others while being transported with a portkey—yes, you can transport soldiers via portkey but they cannot harm anyone while in transit). If a portkey is to transport wizards and witches between two countries, the consent of both countries' Ministry of Magic might be required. This is—as it seems—the equivalent to ASA between Muggle countries.[15]

On to brooms—this is a bit more complicated. In most cases you will have civilian witches and wizards flying on their brooms without any bad intentions. Their seems to be no limit on how far witches and wizards can fly on their brooms. The only constraint will be the witch or wizard's need for sleep, biobreaks, stretching

---

[14]On the scene in the book when Voldemort flew back to Malfoy Manor, rather than apparating: Rowling (2007), Chapter 23: Malfoy Manor. If you don't trust me on the range limit of apparition (mainly due to risk of splinching if the distance is too far), see here: https://twitter.com/jk_rowling/status/799666899021766658.

[15]For more on this please check out Harry Potter Fandom (n.d.). Now, some of you will remember that Newt Scamander still found his way over to France with the help of someone operating illegal portkeys. Again, just because someone is violating the law, does not mean the law ends to exist. More on this in Rowling (2018), Scene 47.

and the like. But what does that mean for travel into other countries? Well, it certainly makes it possible to simply fly into other countries. Should we be concerned? Well, in landlocked countries it certainly becomes likely that witches and wizards simply fly from one country to another without considering anything similar to ASAs. There is no record of this being regulated or any attempts at regulation. So we will have to assume that the wizarding community is comfortable with how civilian witches and wizards travel by broom from country to country.

But what if there are Aurors flying on those brooms? Or if the death eaters decide to move from Britain over to France to expand their sphere of influence? Now we are talking about witches and wizards on brooms with their wands—essentially weapons given the intent—crossing a border. For the Aurors it is possible to argue that they should be handed in the same way as state aircraft or military aircraft as they are essentially state organs, armed, above ground with the ability to inflict damage from the air. Based on the definition of Art. 3 Chicago Convention, any aircraft (which a broom might be in this case) that is used in "military, customs and police services" is seen as a state aircraft.[16] The Aurors would therefore fall under the requirements to receive pre-authorization of other wizarding states before entering them. Which seems about right. But what about the death eaters? Similar rules would likely apply to them.[17] But, let us be honest, given that they would only enter other wizarding states to overthrow their legitimate governments and cause terror among Muggles, half-bloods and Muggle-borns, it is very unlikely that they would properly register with the other wizarding government, receive authorization to enter, or abide by the scope of the authorization.

So while there are similarities between air traffic in Muggle and wizarding world there seem to be far less rules governing air travel in the wizarding world. Rules exist, as Newt Scamander experienced himself when being under the travel ban, but there are ways around it and enforcement seems to be more linked to case-by-case instances, that the relevant Ministries investigate.

References

Bakhtiar HS et al (2016) Air Defence Identification Zone (ADIZ) in international law perspective. J Law Policy Glob 56:16–23
Bourbonniere M, Haeck L (2001) Military aircraft and international law: Chicago Opus 3. J Air Law Commerce 66:885–978
de Leon PM (2022) Introduction to air law, 11th edn. Wolters Kluwer, Alphen aan den Rijn
Harry Potter Fandom (n.d.) Portkey. https://harrypotter.fandom.com/wiki/Portkey. Accessed 27 Dec 2022
Karnitschnig M (2003) Overflight fight: Austria uses antique jets to patrol airspace. WSJ. https://www.wsj.com/articles/SB105121517792169100. Accessed 27 Dec 2022

[16]Go back to read up on this in Sect. 6.2.1 in case you have forgotten.

[17]If you have forgotten how we define state organs, please go back to Sect. 2.2.2.1.

Rowling JK (1998) Harry Potter and the chamber of secrets. Bloomsbury, London
Rowling JK (2007) Harry Potter and the deathly hallows. Bloomsbury, London
Rowling JK (2018) Fantastic beasts: the crimes of Grindelwald. Little, Brown, London
Shaw MN (2017) International law, 8th edn. Cambridge University Press, Cambridge
Whisp K (n.d.) Quidditch through the ages (a work by Rowling JK)

Law of the Sea

7

Abstract

Did you ever wonder what the legal status of Azkaban is? Were you concerned about the fact that the Durmstrang ship just appeared in the lake and questioned who was regulating traffic on the oceans given these ship-shaped submarine? If yes, this is your chapter. We will look into the basics of law of the sea and assess what constitutes an island, what rights states have in the waters surrounding their territory and how travel in waters around a state's territory is regulated.

7.1   What Is Law of the Sea?

Imagine the world a few centuries back. The seafaring nations started claiming the high seas as part of their territory.[1] This idea didn't last long. Instead, the idea of open seas and freedom of the high seas became a principle of international law.[2] But not all the water you see out there is considered the high sea or international water. The many intricate stages in between are regulated in law of the sea, in particular in the 1982 UN Convention on the Law of the Sea (UNCLOS).[3]

Under law of the sea there are many different types of waters or structures in the waters—we will focus on only a few here. Internal waters (imagine lakes or rivers, such as the lake close to Hogwarts) do not lead to any legal claims as they are already covered as part of the sovereign territory of the state.[4] EEZs create rights especially linked to the exploitation of marine resources in the 200 nautical miles from the

---

[1] Yes, this happened. Read more on this approach by the Portuguese and the response by Grotius in Shaw (2017), p. 410.

[2] Shaw (2017), pp. 410 f.

[3] https://www.un.org/depts/los/convention_agreements/texts/unclos/unclos_e.pdf.

[4] Shaw (2017), pp. 412–413.

baselines (Art. 57 ff. UNCLOS).[5] Islands as defined in Art. 121 (1) UNCLOS are seen as part of the territory of a state and create an additional EEZ claim around them (yes, an additional 200 nautical miles radius for resource exploration, remember this for the next section). There are many more different types of waters and legal constructs (e.g., baselines, bays, continental shelves, archipelagic states, international straits, contiguous zones, high seas, international seabed),[6] but we will focus on EEZ, islands and internal waters as they have most relevance for the wizarding world.

Art. 121 UNCLOS

1. An island is a naturally formed area of land, surrounded by water, which is above water at high tide.
2. Except as provided for in paragraph 3, the territorial sea, the contiguous zone, the exclusive economic zone and the continental shelf of an island are determined in accordance with the provisions of this Convention applicable to other land territory.
3. Rocks which cannot sustain human habitation or economic life of their own shall have no exclusive economic zone or continental shelf.

7.2   The Status of the Azkaban Island: Island or Not?

In a previous chapter we talked about the wizarding prison Azkaban.[7] The question we aim to answer is whether the island housing Azkaban would be considered an island. If yes, this would lead to claims such as an EEZ for the wizarding world surrounding Azkaban. While we are not sure of the maritime resources in the waters around Azkaban (some magical seaweed maybe?), no Muggle or witch and wizard has ever shied away from rights to exploit something. So let us see whether there would be legal grounds for it.

As highlighted just before this, an island is a "naturally formed area of land, surrounded by water, which is above water at high tide" (Art. 121 (1) UNCLOS). The island housing Azkaban is described as being an island in the North Sea.[8] It appears to be above water, even at high tide, and houses the wizarding prison Azkaban. It therefore appears to be able to sustain human habitation, although habitation is certainly a stretch when talking about the conditions at Azkaban. Based on the depiction in the movies, nothing appears to grow on the island. Yet, this is not a prerequisite for something to be considered an island.

---

[5] More on this in Shaw (2017), pp. 431 ff.

[6] Yes, I'm just showing off now—but you can read more on all of these in Shaw (2017), pp. 410–482.

[7] In case you have forgotten, please go back here: Sect. 3.6.2.

[8] Rowling (2015), Azkaban.

Based on the information available, we have to assume that the island on which Azkaban is situated would qualify as an island. This also means that around this island the wizarding world would have a 200 nautical mile radius of EEZ, in which it has the right to exploit resources, such as magical seaweed. But what if this overlaps with the EEZ of Muggle Britain? Well, this would not be the first time. There are many cases in which EEZs overlap. In these cases, there are three scenarios. Either, states decide to move ahead and jointly exploit resources in the area that overlaps (the grown-up solution). Or they engage in legal battle to determine which state has which rights (the grown-up but not used to sharing solution). Or they try to exploit as much resources on their own before the other state has a chance to react (the Dudley solution).[9]

7.3 Maritime Travel: Or How Did the Durmstrang Ship Get to Hogwarts?

Last but not least, let us look at the way of travel via sea in the wizarding world. There is limited insight into ships that wizards use (unless they rely on ships as Newt Scamander did). But the one example that stands out is the Durmstrang ship. The magical ship appeared in the lake on Hogwarts grounds for the Triwizard Tournament.[10] At least when on the grounds (or more accurately in the lake) of Hogwarts the ship was in the internal waters of the British wizarding world. This qualifies as territorial waters.

Art. 20 UNCLOS

In the territorial sea, submarines and other underwater vehicles are required to navigate on the surface and to show their flag.

Now in our world, the closest equivalent to the Durmstrang ship is likely a submarine (given that the ship disappeared in the water). Based on Art. 20 UNCLOS, the ship would have been required to navigate on the surface. It clearly did not do that. Instead, it even fires off its canons—although this is in all fairness only done as a salute and not as a threatening gesture towards anyone around. And even worse, it was in internal waters (lake or fjord, not just territorial waters off the coast).

At first sight, this does seem like a clear violation of Art. 20 UNCLOS as the submarine was clearly not navigating on the surface. This does, however, not immediately have to be a violation of Art. 20 UNCLOS. It is possible that the British Ministry of Magic has agreed with the ship navigating below the surface. The other scenario is—and we simply do not have enough facts to be able to make a final

---

[9]For more on these different types of conflict resolution: Shaw (2017), pp. 431 ff.

[10]More on this in Rowling (2000), Chapter 15: Beauxbatons and Durmstrang.

assessment—that there was no real navigation under water as the ship was using magical means to disappear in one large body of water (near Hogwarts) and reappear in another (close to Durmstrang). But this is pure speculation. What is clear is that there was no protest despite officials from the British Ministry of Magic being on site, so we will work with the assumption that this did not constitute a real violation of the law of the sea.

Let us ignore the moment in which the Durmstrang ship was in that lake/fjord for a moment and think about how it got there. If there is no magical way to transport from that lake/fjord to another one closer to Durmstrang, the assumption is that the ship must have travelled to the coast of Scotland and then through the North Sea back home. What about the transit in coastal areas of Scotland? Again, UNCLOS is there to help.

Art. 17 UNCLOS

Subject to this Convention, ships of all States, whether coastal or land-locked, enjoy the right of innocent passage through the territorial sea.

To be clear, Art. 17 UNCLOS refers to passage through the territorial sea. This specifically excludes the option of entering internal waters.[11] So the trip down the fjord to the Hogwarts lake is—as discussed—in all likelihood an exception granted by the British Ministry of Magic for the purpose of the Triwizard Tournament. But what about all the other coast states on the journey home? In general, this would fall under the right of innocent passage. Again, as the ship is *de facto* functioning like a submarine, it would have to navigate on the surface (see Art. 20 UNCLOS). This would not necessarily be a problem, as it is, well, a ship. The more urgent question is how to deal with the fact that this ship has functioning cannons on board. The innocent passage of warships is a more contentious topic.[12] Based on the majority opinion, even warships would be allowed the right for innocent passage, as long as they do not use their weapons or launch aircrafts or military devices.[13]

So to sum it up, even if the magical transportation option from lake to lake were to fail, there is an option for the Durmstrang students to return home. It would, however, require constraint while they are navigating through the territorial waters of other states. No showing off the canons and also no hiding below the surface. But as long as the Durmstrang ship appears like a more modern and functioning version of the Gorch Fock, all should be fine.[14]

There are, and this will be no surprise, many, many more intricate questions linked to law of the sea. But given the context of the wizarding world the two topics

---

[11] Sohn (2010), p. 213.

[12] ibid., pp. 220 ff.

[13] ibid., p. 222.

[14] If you don't get this reference, read up on it here: https://www.dw.com/en/germany-gorch-fock-training-ship-returns-to-service/a-59359547.

discussed seemed most pressing. For any issues beyond this, there is plenty of useful literature out there that can satisfy your curiosity.[15]

References

Rowling JK (2000) Harry Potter and the goblet of fire. Bloomsbury, London

Rowling JK (2015) Azkaban. https://www.wizardingworld.com/writing-by-jk-rowling/azkaban. Accessed 10 Dec 2022

Shaw MN (2017) International law, 8th edn. Cambridge University Press, Cambridge

Sohn L et al (2010) Law of the sea in a nutshell, 2nd edn. West Publishing, St. Paul

---

[15] Sohn (2010); Shaw (2017), pp. 410–482.